"Its drilled into any restaurateurs head its all about the food and it is, but without cashflow the kitchen lights go out quick. Joey explains the bottomline of the financial side of the business helping entrepreneurs make good profits with good food."

Creed Ford
CEO
Fired Up Inc.

"A great read for any one 'moving up' in the food and beverage business. A must read for veteran managers."

E. Gene Street
Chairman of the Board
Consolidated Restaurant Operations, INC.

"Great insight from a great operator. Zapoli takes the mystery out of making money and does so in a clear and convincing way. This read can make a real difference to anyone planning a career in the restaurant industry."

Dick Frank
CEO
Chuck E. Cheese

D1114359

"Zapoli is one of those increasingly rare breed of operators who combine passion for the guest experience with a financial skill set crucial to concept inception and growth. This book is a smart read for the new manager."

David Lory
Franchise Business Consultant
Dickey's Barbecue Restaurant's

"Zapoli is a proven restaurant operations executive and his book hits critical areas that are important for restaurant managers and operators to master.
I think his "hands on" understanding of the subject matter is obvious and new as well as experienced restaurant operators can sharpen their skills by studying the methods outlined in the book. As a former "accountant", I give Zapoli's book "two thumbs up".

Ken Myres
Vice President, Franchise Development
Tony Roma's

"A great tool for someone new to the industry as well as experienced operators who want to know how restaurant accounting really works."

Larry Lavine
(Founder of Chili's)
President
Turtle creek Restaurants

How to Succeed in the Restaurant Business

How to Succeed in the Restaurant Business

Crunching Numbers—Now That's the Bottom Line!

Joseph Robert Zapoli

iUniverse, Inc.

New York Lincoln Shanghai

How to Succeed in the Restaurant Business
Crunching Numbers—Now That's the Bottom Line!

iUniverse books may be ordered through booksellers or by contacting:

iUniverse
2021 Pine Lake Road, Suite 100
Lincoln, NE 68512
www.iuniverse.com
1-800-Authors (1-800-288-4677)

Library of Congress Control Number: 2003097933

The images used herein are obtained from the artist, Kiffany Wood @ 8105 Pacific, Frisco, TX 75035. All Rights Reserved.
This work contains the opinions and ideas of the author. It is intended to provide helpful and informative material on the subjects addressed in this publication.

ISBN-13: 978-0-595-35167-1 (pbk)
ISBN-13: 978-0-595-79866-7 (ebk)
ISBN-10: 0-595-35167-0 (pbk)
ISBN-10: 0-595-79866-7 (ebk)

Printed in the United States of America

I dedicate this book to my father, James Zapoli, who, before passing away in 1998, not only taught me how important it is to understand budgeting and number crunching in your business but how important it is in your personal life as well.

Contents

Preface

I have been in the restaurant business for over seventeen years, and I have managed some of the biggest restaurant chains of today. Through my more than seventeen years, I have been fortunate enough to open fourteen restaurants with seven different major companies. All seven companies are still around and operating to this day. In five out of the seven companies, I have been a general manager and utilized all of the tools I have laid out in this book. Therefore, not only do I know these methods work, but I also know that they have helped me and my managers become successful.

In my years of management, I have seen one basic problem continually burden all levels of management, and sometimes even the owners; I am talking about number crunching. Do you know the number one reason why restaurants go out of business? They go out of business because the people managing the restaurants cannot (or do not know how to) manage their bottom line profits. I have found that most managers shy away from numbers. In talking to some of my past managers, they say they pretend to know the numbers so they can get by, and they choose not to crunch the numbers because it will only show how little they know. How scary is that? It does not take common sense to realize that the more managers that choose not to learn how to crunch numbers, the higher the number of restaurants that go under each year.

A Profit and Loss Statement (P&L) is a basic financial statement in the restaurant industry. Restaurant managers with P&L (number crunching) knowledge are in high demand in this industry. Managers without the knowledge could be making from $30,000 to $40,000, whereas those with the knowledge can start out making from $40,000 to $60,000 and more (depending on one's experience).

Let us address the need to read and really understand this book. If you are a restaurant manager now, plan to be a restaurant manager, or if you own your own restaurant or plan to, you need to make sure you know how to control your cost from the beginning. There are thousands of restaurants in the nation, and each one of them has, on average, four managers per unit. Half, if not more of the managers I have worked with, are just getting by without the right knowledge to make money for the restaurant, as well as themselves. On average, restaurants only make four cents on every dollar coming into the restaurant. If you don't have the knowledge of budgets, cost of sales, ordering and receiving, declining budgets, forecast cost, ideal cost, P&L, etcetera, then it becomes very difficult to make any profit from four cents.

I started writing this book more as a workbook for my immediate management team. Something they could reference from time to time when they had some trouble. I always felt that the more people in the restaurant that have the same awareness that I do, the better. Before writing the workbook, I decided to go to the local bookstore and see if there were some books already published that might help my managers. To my surprise, there were very few books on the "numbers side" of a restaurant. When you do find a book on restaurants, it seems to move quickly through and hit only the surface of budgeting or cost-controlling issues. I picked up a few of these books and was amazed at their approach. The books seemed to be written by people who received an accounting degree and used every technical term they could find. In addition, when I read further into the books, I got a sense that these authors may not have even managed a restaurant before. That is when I decided to write something myself. I told myself I wanted to make it easy to understand. I found a way to break down the number-crunching issues and was able to relate with in-store scenarios and, sometimes, the managers' own personal life. One would not be able to make it in one's own personal life without some crunching of numbers at home.

After giving my managers this workbook I had created, we all noticed some significant improvements in comprehension of budgets and ways to control the dollars being spent in the restaurant. The thing that helped the most, they said, was how it broke down problems into simple examples and explanations. I wrote the workbook and this book as if I were sitting down in a managerial meeting or with my managers one on one and explaining how to control the bottom line.

Have you ever wondered how a restaurant that has great food and great service can go out of business? Maybe you have questioned why some restaurants serve the same items on the menu as the more expensive restaurants do, but have lower menu prices. Perhaps you have seen how some restaurants run without bussers while others run with three or four and yet do the same volume. Have you questioned how and why restaurants that are doing great volume do not always bring in a great return? Or sometimes it could be the same question anyone in the restaurant business has asked, "How do I increase my bottom line in order to put more money in my pocket?" If you hold a position in a restaurant or, more importantly, if you own a restaurant, there are undoubtedly plenty of questions like these about the restaurant business that you should constantly ask yourself. Finally, here is the book that will shed some light on these areas and answer most, if not all, of your questions.

With the recent surge in the restaurant population, it may seem like a restaurant can be found on almost every corner. The competition is intense. The convenience of having everything from Chinese, Japanese, Mexican, Indian, and Italian to burgers and fries within a short distance from home is taken for granted. Less than thirty years ago, a restaurant was not always in a convenient place. The ones that provided the food you wanted and the service you required usually took time to get to. Back then when you went out for a steak, that was all the restaurant would serve. Now, some restaurants offer Mexican, Chinese, and Italian all in one place!

Convenience became such a necessity in the restaurant industry that fast food places evolved. Who would have thought fifty years ago that you could drive up to a side of a building, choose from a menu detailing an array of foods, place your order into a box, drive up to a window, and receive your food in about five minutes? Sure, you are not getting the same quality service and great food, but the convenience cannot be beat.

Unfortunately, convenience has almost become as important to consumers as great food and outstanding service. It is easy to see that convenience is high on the priority list when we now have food delivery service replacing the experience of dining out. Not only are restaurants getting in on home delivery, but so are grocery stores as well. With convenience like that, why would anyone venture away from home?

Families have changed; gone are the days when the family sat around the dinner table with a home-cooked meal. Due to the increase in and, in some cases, necessity of dual income families, single-parent homes, and all of the running around to get the kids from the daycare to soccer practice, who has time to cook? Many families are turning to dining out for family meals. Well, imagine a place where you could go and have a different experience than what you are used to getting at home or work. I am talking about a place where you are greeted with a big smile and a warm welcome. Once inside the restaurant, you are then seated in a comfortable chair and given a menu that gives them a choice of several different drinks and food items. If you compared this to my house, I get the choice of leftovers or some canned items. All you have to do in a restaurant is kick back and be waited on. After you order, the food and drinks are delivered to your table. No need to worry about getting up for refills; that is done without you lifting a finger. If something is spilled, dropped, or broken, you do not even have to worry. After you have eaten your meal, you get a choice of dessert and after-dinner drinks. There is no need to worry about cleaning plates, throwing away trash, or clearing the table. All of this is done with a smile and all in exchange for a few pieces of green cloth we call money.

If you are like my wife and me, you will find yourself in a restaurant almost every night of the week. We would rather have someone else making the meal and doing the dishes. We both work until 7:00 PM, and the last thing we feel like doing is wasting our quality time chopping, dicing, mixing, cooking, and cleaning.

Since there are many people who think the same as we do, why is it that restaurants are not packed on a nightly basis? Competition! There are hundreds of restaurants to choose from. In Dallas, Texas, alone, there are over 2,500 restaurants opened every year. Due to the over-abundance of restaurants, it is difficult for the owners to stay in business when everyone else is doing the same thing—namely, providing good food, good service, atmosphere, and location.

When a restaurant has these key things in place already and still finds it hard to stay profitable, then it is time to start asking a few of the questions I mentioned earlier.

Restaurants are becoming harder and harder to manage than ever before. With all that is involved in opening a restaurant, it is surprising that so many are opening every day. Anyone from famous movie stars like Arnold Schwarzenegger and Bruce Willis to the average Joe down the street is getting in on this growing industry. The restaurant business is a gamble. What makes some successful and others unsuccessful? The restaurant business is not prejudiced by any means. Whether you are famous or not, we all have the same chance of making a restaurant successful.

Chapter One:

"We used to say that Williams was 'lazy' -
now we think of him as 'motivationally challenged.'"

Introduction

In order to know how to increase the bottom line, one must first know what the bottom line is and why it is so important. The *bottom line* equals the series of numbers generated collectively that total the amount of expenses paid in order to run the business for a certain period. These numbers are then balanced against the amount of total revenue and devised in a way to give the net profit or loss on a percentage ratio equaling cents to the dollar. The bottom line can be located on the last line of the P&L or the budget. Although this sounds a little complicated, it is actually quite simple and will be broken down and explained in full detail throughout this book. The bottom line is your balance, or net profit or loss, at the end of any given period. It is just like balancing your checkbook at home. You constantly write down what you put into the account and take out. While doing so, you also add and subtract what you have in the account to give you an ending balance. How do you know when you have made a mistake? Usually you cross-reference your checkbook with the bank statement you receive. Therefore, no matter what, you always know where your account balance stands or you can question anything that may look out of place, because you have been watching it and you know when a wrong amount has been entered. The reason why numbers are so important to your business is the simple fact that the numbers do not lie. Even if the food and bar inventories were done incorrectly, or if some employees forgot to clock in, numbers do not lie. How can this be? If you are always watching and controlling (crunching) the numbers and someone else was to implement something wrong, you would be able to catch it and correct it, as you would with your own checkbook. Of course, in order to do this you will have to become better acquainted with numbers and understand what to look for.

Unfortunately, many people running a business do not understand number crunching and are easily turned away from ever having to learn. The reality of crunching numbers, once understood, becomes addictive, challenging, and—eventually—enjoyable.

Through my years of managing some of the largest and most successful restaurants in the nation, I have seen different ways in which these companies structure their bottom line in order to find their profit for certain periods. I have found, that although companies may vary the terminology (P&L, bottom line, profit margin, below-the-line profits, ending return, etc.), the way they calculate their various costs are the same. If you ever switch to a different restaurant company you will find that the menu has changed, the atmosphere is different, and the uniforms are new. But things you will not find different are the ways in which they calculate the numbers. One of the few exceptions seems to be the way each restaurant calculates their depreciation. I have seen some companies do a better job than others when it comes to writing in all their depreciation. The company's accountant should be the one regulating the depreciation. The accountant takes into consideration the value of the building and all of its contents. Depreciation is just that. Just like when you buy a car—once you drive it off the lot, it will begin to depreciate. This holds true in the restaurant business on almost everything in your restaurant. Once you have bought an item or building, it starts to lose its value. As they lose value, you must account for that as a loss on your P&L. When you are looking at depreciation, you are not looking at a number that actually takes cash out of your restaurant, but one that makes up for the lost value of your restaurant. With depreciation in the P&L, the bottom of the P&L is called your *store profit*. If you wanted to know exactly how much cash you had at the end of a month you would not include the depreciation in the P&L. This is called Cash on Cash. Not all budgets and P&Ls will look the same. Depending on the company running the restaurant, some budgets will be broken out into every category known to restaurants. Others may have the basics listed on the budget and have the subcategories built into them. Some restaurants crunch numbers a little harder than others, and you may only be exposed to certain sections of the P&L. Do not let this fool you. The budget I refer to in this book may not look like anything you have seen. I just want you to understand how to crunch the numbers and then relate it back to your own budget. The reason you need to know how to crunch numbers now is so you can start understanding the other 50% of your job. In addition, the only way you will be promoted or will be able to maintain the restaurant you own is by understanding how to control the numbers.

When I say 50% of managing a restaurant is focused on numbers, I am talking about the *50% theory.* The other 50% should be focused on what you are probably already doing—taking care of the guest. When you are taking care of the guest, you in turn take care of your top line (your revenue). The more sales you have, the easier it is to make money on the bottom line. If you have great revenue, you can get away with more spoilage, comps, labor, and other categories. When you do not have great revenue, you need to control your dollars even more. If you relate this to your own personal spending, you could say the difference would be between a promotion and demotion. With a promotion, you can spend a little more on clothes and dining out and still pay all your normal bills. With a demotion, you would need to cut back on buying clothes and dining out so that you have money to pay your normal bills. Your normal bills in your personal life are called fixed cost. Fixed cost can also be found in a restaurant. *Fixed cost* refers to any amount of dollars spent during a given period on a particular item or category that remains standard. An example of fixed cost in a restaurant would be your pest control, alarm company, rental equipment, landscaping, and any other item or category for which your total bill amount does not change. An example of this in your personal life would be your car payment, insurance, or the cable bill. In the restaurant business, you must have a good balance between the top line and the bottom line. As a manager, this means 50% of the focus must be on operations and 50% on controlling costs.

An important point needs to be made here. I consider this the 50% theory because it provides an even balance between taking care of the customer and taking care of the restaurant. Without one or the other, you will fail. If you want to stay in business, your focus must always be 50% on the customer and 50% on the numbers. Say that you would rather put this book down and ignore the 50% theory because you believe that if you take care of the guest, the numbers will take care of themselves. This can be true in some cases, but for most restaurants, *numbers never just happen; you create them* every day. That's right, every day. You control the numbers in the way you want. On the flip side, if you control the numbers too much and start to cut down on portion size, raise menu prices, and cut your labor down so low you end up providing poor service, you will lose your guests, and your revenue will decline. When your revenue declines, your bottom line profits will decline, as well. Let me give you another example: Both my wife and I work and make money to split the bills we have each month. Any money left over goes directly into our savings account. If my wife decided to stop working, we would have less income (revenue) with which to pay the bills. This would result in less or no money to put into the savings account. The same would happen in the restaurant if the revenue were to decline. However, if your revenue declines, it means that, for the most part, you do not have to spend as much money buying product and supplies because you will not need them. However, you will still have noncontrollable bills to pay, like your lease, any rented equipment, insurance, taxes, and so forth, and these will not decline even if your revenue does. The result will be less or no money added to the bottom line for profit. This is why it is crucial that you understand the 50% theory before you move on.

Through the years, I have heard many excuses about why department managers cannot maintain a declining budget and help with crunching numbers. Excuses like, "I don't have enough time," or "I have so much other stuff to do." My guess would be, they just do not know how to crunch numbers or they are embarrassed or afraid to say it. The number-crunching part of the 50% theory only takes a little time and practice to understand and maintain, *yet this solution is the number one reason restaurants go out of business.*

Unfortunately, too many entrepreneurs feel that if they can serve a group of people in their own home or even cater a small event, they can run a restaurant. The truth about restaurants that people do not realize is that there is very little money to be made. It's true! In fact, restaurants, on average, only profit four cents on every dollar. How could this be? How can there be people who own restaurants that become millionaires if they only make four cents on the dollar? Remember the old adage, "It takes money to make money." In order to become a millionaire in the restaurant industry, there has to be a big investment, low overhead, and room to expand to different locations.

The restaurant industry is not for those who are looking to get rich quick. It takes long hours and a lot of hard work just to stay profitable. On top of not making a lot of money, your chances of failure are extremely high. Look at all the cost that it takes to open and maintain a restaurant. First, you will need to find a location in which to build or purchase, which in turn results in huge up-front cost. You may opt to do a leasehold agreement. If you build your own place, you will have a lot of up-front cost, and it will take you close to eight months or more from start to finish. This time is so varied due to city regulations, licenses, permits, and Mother Nature. If you opt to lease, you will have a lower up-front cost and open the restaurant in a much quicker time.

Now that you have your place, you may need lights, gas, air-conditioning, heat, kitchen equipment, dishes, silverware, paint, wallpaper, tables, chairs, phones, a fax machine, a copier, a computer, a hood system, stainless steel for your wait stations and kitchen areas, paper products, cleaning chemicals, menus, uniforms, office supplies, stock, people to greet your guest coming in, people to serve your guest, bartenders, kitchen employees, and management to watch over all of this—and these are just the basics. You can up the cost if it is a theme restaurant that requires special items for the decor. Finally, licenses and permits are required just about anywhere you open up for business. Therefore, as you can see, there are many ways to lose profit in a restaurant if you do not have the 50% theory in place before you even open your doors.

The first step in crunching numbers is to establish *break points*. Break points equal the dollar amount in sales revenue the restaurant must hit in order to stay profitable. When I say *must* hit, I mean there are no other options without altering the rest of the budget. For example, if we were talking about a normal casual restaurant and we said your kitchen labor percentage for Monday is budgeted at 9.5%. In the kitchen you cannot run with less than five employees on each lunch and dinner shift. This is the bare minimum number of employees in the kitchen to cover all stations (you may have employees covering two stations on some shifts) and maximize prep. When you do less than $6,000 in sales revenue, your labor percentage goes over 9.5%. Therefore, in order for your kitchen labor to be at 9.5%, the break point will be $6,000 for Monday. You can always do more in sales, but, if you do any less, you will not be able to hit your labor percentage. This in turn will shrink your profitability. The break point is gotten when you calculate the lowest possible labor force the kitchen can have and still run productively and efficiently. Take that labor (for this example we are saying we have to run with at least ten people to run productively and efficiently), add the amount of hours used in the kitchen that those ten people worked on that day, and multiply it by the average wage. Once you have the total, divide this by the percentage you want to hit and this will give you the revenue break point. (For example, the fewest kitchen employees you can run with on a Monday is ten. On average, each employee makes $9.50 an hour and works six hours.

Then take your ten employees, multiply this by the $9.50 an hour that, on average, they make, and then multiply this by the six hours they worked.

    10.0 (least amount of employees you can run with)
  x   9.5 (average hourly labor)
    $95.00 $95
                      x   6 (average hours worked by the employees)
                      $570

Now, you can take this ending number of $570 and divide this by 9.5%, which is the target you want your kitchen labor to be at, and you will reach your revenue break point of $6,000.

    $570.00 (cost from above)
  ÷   .095 (what is budgeted for kitchen labor)
    $6,000.00

Now, if you are not hitting the revenue that you have found to be your break point, and feel you will never be able to reach this revenue, then you need to up your kitchen labor percentage in your budget and look to cut back in other areas. Look at this as if you are making the same salary you have been making before you bought a newer and more expensive car. Since you are putting more money toward your new car payment, you may have to adjust your personal spending in other areas. Remember, the break point is the revenue that *must* be hit. *Finding the break point, and making everyone aware of it, is imperative to daily operations.* If revenue exceeds the break point, it is much easier to control or maintain the budget. In order to find out who, what, when, where, why, and how you should make the cuts in the restaurant, you must create a budget.

Chapter Two:

"That must be the clown in charge of the budget."

The Budget

Many years ago, my wife and I were getting ready to go out to eat and see a movie when we discovered that neither of us had the money to do so. We stared at one another in disbelief. We both made enough money to know that spending an evening out should never be a problem. However, it was. At first, we started pointing the finger at one another.

"You waste too much money on all the fast food you eat," my wife yelled.

"Well, you spend too much money on little 'project' stuff that you always start but you never finish," I shot back. We went back and forth until we decided we had better see if we had enough money to pay the bills that month. After analyzing the bills, we were back at each other's throats.

This went on for the next half hour, until my wife brought up something that had us both stumped and pondering quietly to ourselves. She asked, "How did our parents do it?" We sat down together and thought about our parents, who had survived on half (or less) the income we had and yet were able to make ends meat. To top it off, they were able to do it raising a house full of kids. How did they do it? How could they survive with so little money? Sure, things were cheaper back then, but my wife and I made over twice what they had, and we had no children at the time.

Still confused, we decided the best way to find out how our parents got by was by asking them. It was then that our parents reminded us that not only was food on the table every night but also that they were able to build up savings accounts for those days when they might not be too sure where dinner would come from. "A savings account?" I exclaimed. My wife and I were doing good to pay the bills, eat, and squeak by for the month, from paycheck to paycheck, much less have money saved up for a rainy day. Now I was really confused. Comparatively speaking, we were failing. They had been around for decades and had made it through the good times and the bad. Yet my wife and I were about to move back into one of our parents' houses if we could not come up with a better way of managing our money.

That is when the solution hit me. Why do some restaurants close down even though they have great food and great service? For the same reason that my wife and I were about to move back in with one of our parents. Whether it is in your everyday life or running a restaurant, you must *manage* your money. I am talking about being in full control of your finances. Manage every cent. Find out where your money is going and where it has been. Keep track of every penny that leaves your wallet, checkbook, purse, savings account, company, and so forth. Once you have a history of your spending, you need to develop a budget. A budget is simply a statement of finances of an entity, whether it's a restaurant or a person, for a period of time, based on expenditures and income during that period. As a planning statement, a budget will enable such an entity to set priorities and monitor progress toward selected goals.

Once we had figured out that a budget was what my wife and I needed, we put our heads together and wrote down all of our expenses. For categories of which we were not exactly sure how much money we might spend (like groceries, eating out, entertainment, etc.), we gave ourselves a certain amount to use on a daily basis. Any time we spent money, we wrote it in the correct category on the budget. If a category needed to be developed for a certain cost, we simply added one and readjusted the budget. It was amazing to us how much money we actually spent. The good news was, we found many areas of our budget in which we could cut our spending, and therefore save a lot. This is the same reason why it is so important for a restaurant to establish and maintain a budget.

In order to create and follow a budget, one must study it in detail—column-by-column, line-by-line—to better understand what it says. First, you will see a full-blown budget, and then we will break it into separate quarters to better understand its constituent parts.

Budgets come in all shapes and sizes and may vary in terminology. The budget that follows will help you understand the fundamentals that are needed to create and maintain a budget. This is by no means the only correct way to maintain a budget, but it will give you a good look at one and make it easier for you when you are creating and maintaining your own. This budget shows different terminology and categories that this company uses. The monthly budget I use here is for an average restaurant and will be easy to understand. This budget represents a restaurant averaging $53,000 in total revenue each week for a five-week period. It is also broken down into more categories than most restaurants will have.

2.1 The Budget

Restaurant Name Here
Budget Form for Income Statement

RESTAURANT:
MONTH:

REVENUE			OTHER EXPENSES		
FOOD	$219,950.00	83.00%	ADVERTISING	$6,000.00	2.26%
			AUTO ALLOWANCE	$0.00	0.00%
LIQUOR	$18,550.00	7.00%	BANK FEES	$250.00	0.09%
BEER	$15,900.00	6.00%	BUILDING SIGNAGE	$220.00	0.08%
WINE	$10,600.00	4.00%	CASH OVER/SHORT	$100.00	0.04%
TOTAL LBW	$45,050.00	17.00%	COMPUTER	$0.00	0.00%
			CASUAL LABOR	$0.00	0.00%
OTHER			CHARGE BACK	$100.00	0.04%
TOTAL REVENUE	$265,000.00	100.00%	CORP. CONTRIBUTION	$750.00	0.28%
			CREDIT CARD FEE	$6,900.00	2.60%
COST OF SALE			CUSTOMER RELATION	$0.00	0.00%
FOOD	$67,084.75	30.50%	DUES AND SUBSCRIPTIONS	$120.00	0.05%
			ENTERTAINMENT	$280.00	0.11%
LIQUOR	$2,226.00	12.00%	FREIGHT AND COURIER	$150.00	0.06%
BEER	$3,339.00	21.00%	GROSS RECEIPT TAX	$3,975.00	1.50%
WINE	$2,438.00	23.00%	ICE	$150.00	0.06%
TOTAL LBW	$8,003.00	17.76%	INSURANCE GENERAL	$2,000.00	0.75%
			LAUNDRY AND UNIFORM	$2,200.00	0.83%
OTHER			MEDICAL COST WC	$2,000.00	0.75%
TOTAL COST OF SALE	$75,087.75	28.34%	OFFICE SUPPLIES	$300.00	0.11%
			PENALTIES	$0.00	0.00%
GROSS PROFIT	$189,912.25	71.67%	PEST CONTROLL	$280.00	0.11%
PAYROLL AND RELATED EXPENSES			PLANT AND LAWN CARE	$450.00	0.17%
LABOR MAINTENACE	$344.50	0.13%	POSTAGE	$40.00	0.02%
LABOR KITCHEN STAFF	$26,500.00	10.00%	PRINTING AND STATIONARY	$80.00	0.03%
LABOR TRAINING KITCHEN	$0.00		PROMOTION	$150.00	0.06%
LABOR WAIT STAFF	$6,890.00	2.60%	REPAIR AND MAINTANCE	$2,000.00	0.75%
LABOR BUS STAFF	$212.00	0.08%	RENT BUILDING	$4,725.00	1.78%
LABOR OYSTER BAR	$0.00	0.00%	RENT EQUIPMENT	$295.00	0.11%
LABOR HOSTESS	$212.00	0.08%	RENT ICE MACHINE	$730.00	0.28%
LABOR BAR	$2,650.00	1.00%	RENT PARKING VALIDATION	$275.00	0.10%
LABOR FRONT MANAGER	$9,275.00	3.50%	RENT OTHER	$150.00	0.06%
LABOR BANQUET RESERV			RENT GE CAPITAL	$500.00	0.19%
LABOR KITCHEN MANAGERS	$9,275.00	3.50%	SECURITY	$420.00	0.16%
LABOR TRAINING MANAGER			SPOILAGE	$250.00	0.09%
LABOR BOOKEEPERS	$689.00	0.26%	SUPPLIES PAPER GOODS	$2,650.00	1.00%
LABOR MANAGER BONUS	$2,650.00	1.00%	SUPPLIES CLEANING	$1,200.00	0.45%
PAYROLL TAXES	$10,070.00	3.80%	SUPPLIES KITCHEN	$775.00	0.29%
INSURANCE GROUP	$901.00	0.34%	SUPPLIES GLASS	$300.00	0.11%
EMPLOYEE BENEFIT PAY	$901.00	0.34%	SUPPLIES SILVERWARE	$300.00	0.11%
MANAGER MEALS	$927.50	0.35%	SUPPLIES CHINA	$500.00	0.19%
EXECUTIVE MEAL	$901.00	0.34%	SUPPLIES MISCELLANEOUS	$300.00	0.11%
EMPLOYEE MEALS 100%	$609.50	0.23%	TAXES TAXES & LICENSES	$428.00	0.16%
EMPLOYEE MEALS 50%	$669.00	0.26%	TAXES PROPERTY	$2,280.00	0.86%
EMPLOYEE BENEFITS	$927.50	0.35%	TELEPHONE & TELEGRAPH	$732.00	0.28%
TOTAL PAYROLL AND RELATED EXPENSES	$74,624.00	28.16%	LIQUOR TAXES	$6,307.00	14.00%
			DEPRECIATION	$12,345.00	4.66%
			UTILITIES	$10,540.00	3.98%
			TOTAL OTHER EXPENSES	$74,497.00	28.11%
			TOTAL EXPENSES	$149,121.00	56.27%
			RESTAURANT LEVEL PROFIT	$40,791.25	15.39%

Let us start by looking at the three columns that make up this budget. Column A simply lists the items or categories in the restaurant that ought to be controlled and maintained throughout the month and year. Column B is in dollars and cents. These dollars-and-cents amounts represent the cash flow coming into the restaurant in terms of revenues and profits (or the cash flow going out of the restaurant in terms of expenses and losses). Column C is the percentage (rounded to tenths of a percent) of money in each related item or category that is coming in or going out of the restaurant.

2.2 Revenue

Column A	Column B	Column C
FOOD	$219,950.00	83.00%
LIQUOR	$18,550.00	7.00%
BEER	$15,900.00	6.00%
WINE	$10,600.00	4.00%
TOTAL LBW	$45,050.00	17.00%
OTHER		
TOTAL REVENUE	$265,000.00	100.00%

Now, take a look at the rows that make up the budget. The first section is called revenue. *Revenue* is the income produced by a given category. Revenue can be found in 2.2 and is the first part of the budget. This first section is simply telling us that we believe the restaurant, based on prior calculations, will be able to generate this amount of cash flow in the given categories. The *total revenue* is the total amount of cash flow projected for a given period of time. For this budget, the period is five weeks. Anything below the total revenue on a budget will be subtracted from that line. Total revenue is similar to the paychecks you receive in a month. This is the money you get to spend and use to pay your fixed bills. When you look at a budget for the restaurant, I want you to think of it in terms of your own expenses. You get your paycheck (total revenue) and then everything beyond this—your car payment, insurance, groceries, and so forth will be subtracted from it. Once you have your total revenue, you can then decide, again based on prior history, what percentage your sales will be in food, liquor, beer, and wine. When you have your percentage for each category, you simply multiply your total revenue by your percentage to calculate what the cash flow will be in the separate categories. If you look at food in 2.1 The Budget, you see that 83% of your total revenue is in this category. Therefore, if you took the total revenue of $265,000 multiplied it by 0.83 you would end up with your cash flow or sales revenue in food of $219,950.

265,000 (budgeted total revenue)

×   .83 (percentage of total revenue devoted to food)

$219,950 (food revenue)

Have you wondered how someone can calculate their total revenue if they have a new restaurant and they have no prior history on which to project these numbers? You already have the tools to be able to calculate this, but you probably didn't know you did. You should know how many tables are in your restaurant, hours you're open in a day, and what your busiest hours of operation will be. (Busy times will vary depending on location, business sector, and demographics. These factors will determine whether you'll be busier in the day, night, or both.) In addition, your p.p.a. (per person average) or your average spend (your p.p.a. and your average spend is the average cost for any one person dining in your restaurant) and that an average table turn time in a restaurant is forty-five minutes. (This time varies with every restaurant, depending on the theme, if you have TV's in the dining area, a game room, a band or show, or something else that might hold the guests' attention.) Well, with these simple facts and figures you do have the tools necessary to calculate your total revenue. All you need now is the formula and some restaurant educated knowledge. The reason for educated knowledge is that when it comes to restaurants, business can be very unpredictable.

To calculate your sales for a nonexistent restaurant, take how many hours it will be open (11:00 AM to 10:00 PM for this example), multiply this by sixty (the minutes in an hour), and divide this by forty-five (the average turn time in minutes).

$$60 \text{ (minutes in an hour)}$$
$$\underline{\times \quad 11} \text{ (hours of operation)}$$
$$660 \qquad 660 \text{ (total to be divided)}$$
$$\underline{\div \quad 45} \text{ (average time in minutes it takes to turn a seat)}$$
$$14.67$$

This tells you that, if every seat were full from the minute you opened until the minute you closed, you would have turned the tables a little less than fifteen times. Realistically, having every seat full from the time of opening, until closing, happens in very few restaurants. This is where your restaurant educated knowledge comes in. Again, depending on location and demographics, your restaurant may be busier at lunch, dinner, or equally busy at both times. You will probably also have to consider what time of year it is in determining how busy you will be (e.g., if your restaurant is in a mall, amusement park, ball park, or ski resort). Once you have calculated the number of times your seats turn, you then multiply it by the number of seats in the restaurant.

For example, let us say that this restaurant will be full 60% of the time; you then take the 60% and multiply it by the 14.67 times that you turn the seats if the restaurant is full from opening to closing.

$$14.67 \text{ (average times the tables turn)}$$
$$\underline{\times \quad .60} \text{ (seats being full 60\% of the time)}$$
$$8.80$$

You now know that when the restaurant is 60% full in any given day, the seats turn almost nine times. Then, take the number of times you turn the seats and multiply it by how many seats you have. The last step in calculating the revenue for any given day in a new restaurant is to take the 8.80 and multiply it by the per person average (p.p.a.).

8.80 (number of times the seats turn if the restaurant is 60% full)

× 100 (number of seats)

880   880

×   12 (p.p.a. in this example)

$10,560 (projected daily revenue)

The way you just calculated the revenue for one day now needs to be calculated for each individual day. Each day's revenue will vary in the number of seat turns the restaurant will have. Once you have calculated each day of the week, add them up and multiply by either four or five, depending on how many weeks are in the period you are calculating the revenue for. Place this on your budget under the total revenue category and then proceed to break the revenue into food, liquor, beer, and wine.

2.3 Cost of Sales

FOOD	$67,084.75	30.50%
LIQUOR	$2,226.00	12.00%
BEER	$3,339.00	21.00%
WINE	$2,438.00	23.00%
TOTAL LBW	$8,003.00	17.76%
OTHER		
TOTAL COST OF SALE	$75,087.75	28.34%

Cost of sales (c.o.s.) refers to the amount of money and percent of revenue it cost, in food, liquor, beer, and wine in order to create the revenue. In simpler terms, you have to spend money to make money, meaning you have to buy food to put food on the menu. Under the cost of sales category, as seen in 2.3, you need to separate the categories into sections, so you can see how much money is needed in each category. You also break them into separate sections so you can track the profits and losses while producing the revenue. On this budget, you can see that you used $67,084.75 in food for the period in order to produce the food revenue of $219,950.00. You use the percentage in this area in order to track the stability of this category. It is always a good idea to do weekly or bimonthly inventories of all your goods that affect your cost of sales. If the percentage rises or falls within the month, it tells you that, sometime during the month, the way you sold your food (how much you sold an item for, or what you were selling it for that month, or how much of each item was sold) or the way in which you control your food (food spoilage, theft, invoicing issues, or the amount of food waste) was altered in one way or another. Many companies do weekly c.o.s. inventories to see where they stand in comparison to their budget. A good thing to remember is that the higher the percentages are, the worse you are doing. The way to find the food cost of a particular item can take time to find and be very involved. *Food cost* is taking how much an item cost to make, and dividing it by how much it sells for on the menu. Finding out the cost of any menu item can be complicated once you take into consideration every measured ingredient in a recipe and pricing out accordingly. Some restaurants go as far as adding the garnish for the plate, the grease that was used if it was fried, the amount of labor and time it took to prep the item, and so on.

If a menu item costs $4.25 to make and you sell this item on the menu for $16.00, the food cost for this single item is 27%.

$$4.25 \text{ (cost of making the product)}$$
$$\div \quad \underline{16} \text{ (the menu price)}$$
$$.27 \text{ (food cost in percentage)}$$

What does this mean? Well, food cost (as well as liquor, beer, and wine cost) will be discussed in a later chapter. However, for now, let us just take steps to better understand the budget before you go rushing too far ahead. As with food, you use the same formulas to find liquor, beer, and wine cost. Again, these categories are separate, so you may watch your progress for gains and losses in each.

2.4 Payroll and Related Expenses

LABOR MAINTENACE	$344.50	0.13%
LABOR KITCHEN STAFF	$26,500.00	10.00%
LABOR TRAINING KITCHEN	$0.00	
LABOR WAIT STAFF	$6,890.00	2.60%
LABOR BUS STAFF	$212.00	0.08%
LABOR OYSTER BAR	$0.00	0.00%
LABOR HOSTESS	$212.00	0.08%
LABOR BAR	$2,650.00	1.00%
LABOR FRONT MANAGER	$9,275.00	3.50%
LABOR BANQUET RESERV		
LABOR KITCHEN MANAGERS	$9,275.00	3.50%
LABOR TRAINING MANAGER		
LABOR BOOKEEPERS	$689.00	0.26%
LABOR MANAGER BONUS	$2,650.00	1.00%
PAYROLL TAXES	$10,070.00	3.80%
INSURANCE GROUP	$901.00	0.34%
EMPLOYEE BENEFIT PAY	$901.00	0.34%
MANAGER MEALS	$927.50	0.35%
EXECUTIVE MEAL	$901.00	0.34%
EMPLOYEE MEALS 100%	$609.50	0.23%
EMPLOYEE MEALS 50%	$689.00	0.26%
EMPLOYEE BENEFITS	$927.50	0.35%
TOTAL PAYROLL AND RELATED EXPENSES	$74,624.00	28.16%

Payroll and related expenses refers to every person and position that works for and is paid by the restaurant. Many of the categories found in 2.4 may be labor categories that will not pertain to your restaurant. In the same respect, there may be other labor categories that you will need to add. Remember, this is a hypothetical budget. The numbers and percentages you see in 2.4 are obviously not set in stone. In other words, budgeted labor percentages and dollars are all based on the individual restaurant's needs and desires. So how is it that some restaurants run without any bussers on a shift and some restaurants run with three or four and yet do the same volume? Each restaurant has its own philosophy on operations. Some feel they would rather put fewer dollars and percentage loss toward bussers and use that money and percentage in another labor category. On the other hand, some restaurants view bussers as a priority, even taking a great deal of dollars and percentage loss in the busser category in order for their restaurant to thrive. I will get into labor and scheduling in a later chapter.

In the next section, I have included several categories (e.g., advertising, corporate expense, and depreciation) that many companies will put below the line. *Below the line* refers to any expenses regulated by corporate that are usually not shown on a budget but will be shown on the profit-and-loss statement to get the true bottom line.

2.5 Controllables and Noncontrollables

OTHER EXPENSES

ADVERTISING	$6,000.00	2.26%
AUTO ALLOWANCE	$0.00	0.00%
BANK FEES	$250.00	0.09%
BUILDING SIGNAGE	$220.00	0.08%
CASH OVER/SHORT	$100.00	0.04%
COMPUTER	$0.00	0.00%
CASUAL LABOR	$0.00	0.00%
CHARGE BACK	$100.00	0.04%
CORP. CONTRIBUTION	$750.00	0.28%
CREDIT CARD FEE	$6,900.00	2.60%
CUSTOMER RELATION	$0.00	0.00%
DUES AND SUBSCRIPTIONS	$120.00	0.05%
ENTERTAINMENT	$280.00	0.11%
FREIGHT AND COURIER	$150.00	0.06%
GROSS RECEIPT TAX	$3,975.00	1.50%
ICE	$150.00	0.06%
INSURANCE GENERAL	$2,000.00	0.75%
LAUNDRY AND UNIFORM	$2,200.00	0.83%
MEDICAL COST WC	$2,000.00	0.75%
OFFICE SUPPLIES	$300.00	0.11%
PENALTIES	$0.00	0.00%
PEST CONTROLL	$280.00	0.11%
PLANT AND LAWN CARE	$450.00	0.17%
POSTAGE	$40.00	0.02%
PRINTING AND STATIONARY	$80.00	0.03%
PROMOTION	$150.00	0.06%
REPAIR AND MAINTANCE	$2,000.00	0.75%
RENT BUILDING	$4,725.00	1.78%
RENT EQUIPMENT	$295.00	0.11%
RENT ICE MACHINE	$730.00	0.28%
RENT PARKING VALIDATION	$275.00	0.10%
RENT OTHER	$150.00	0.06%
RENT GE CAPITAL	$500.00	0.19%
SECURITY	$420.00	0.16%
SPOILAGE	$250.00	0.09%
SUPPLIES PAPER GOODS	$2,650.00	1.00%
SUPPLIES CLEANING	$1,200.00	0.45%
SUPPLIES KITCHEN	$775.00	0.29%
SUPPLIES GLASS	$300.00	0.11%
SUPPLIES SILVERWARE	$300.00	0.11%
SUPPLIES CHINA	$500.00	0.19%
SUPPLIES MISCELLANEOUS	$300.00	0.11%
TAXES TAXES & LICENSES	$428.00	0.16%
TAXES PROPERTY	$2,280.00	0.86%
TELEPHONE & TELEGRAPH	$732.00	0.28%
LIQUOR TAXES	$6,307.00	14.00%
DEPRECIATION	$12,345.00	4.66%
UTILITIES	$10,540.00	3.98%
TOTAL OTHER EXPENSES	$74,497.00	28.11%

Controllables and noncontrollables are expenses in a restaurant that are not included in the food cost or labor cost categories and deal with items that can be controlled as well as set, constant items that cannot be controlled by management. Some examples of items that a management team can control are linen, paper supplies, china, and silverware cost. Now, I know you're probably saying, "How can I control linen, paper, and so on? If I need these items, then I need these items. How is that controlling?" Well, you would be right to say that if you need these items, then you have to purchase them or your restaurant will not function properly. The controlling part of these items comes before the purchase, during the delivery, and after it is in the restaurant.

Picture what would happen if the management team decided to have the linen in an area accessible to everyone. They just throw the linen up on a shelf in the kitchen without any organization. Employees could use as much as they felt necessary. When it comes time to order, it becomes tough to see whether you have enough or too little. This is a restaurant manager's nightmare. If this were the case, the restaurant would constantly be out of linen or have way too much on hand and drive up the budget. Now, picture your linen locked in a cage. The only time the cage is opened is by management. You have par levels set for your linen and your linen is organized. When you place your order, you look at the kitchen schedule and count out how many employees you will have from the time of that delivery to the next time you will get a delivery. Then you only order the amount of aprons and towels it will take to give each person their allotted number of each item. When the linen comes in, it is separated into days and shifts. Each kitchen employee receives their aprons and towels for their shift, the bussers and bartenders are given theirs, and the servers get theirs. Any other use of the linen has to be approved through a manager. Once all this is separated, the management team hands out the linen prior to the start of the shift. If you and the other managers are tracking where every piece of linen goes and how many times it is used before being discarded, you are controlling your cost. This is not the only way to control linen, but it gets the idea across that when budgeting controllables and noncontrollables, you have to decide whether the item you are budgeting can be controlled. If it can be controlled, are you doing everything possible to control it?

Some restaurants budget their electric/AC as a controllable. That's right. As a manager, you control when you turn on all the lights, heavy kitchen equipment, and outside lights. A good rule of thumb is to have your electric company come out and show you how you could save money on your electric bill. Unbelievably, your electric company wants you to use less energy, and they can show you how. In some areas, when heavy kitchen equipment is turned on all at once, it will cause a big surge, which will increase your electric bill. Some electric companies regulate your bill by your highest energy surge every fifteen minutes. If you flip on all of your equipment within a fifteen-minute period, you could be charged that amount of energy for the rest of the day, or even the rest of the month. Again, it is always a good idea to get your electric company to come out and help.

Have you thought about your trash pick-up as a controllable? The difference between not controlling the situation by letting employees throw whole boxes into the dumpster and by controlling it and making them break and even stomp the boxes down before throwing them inside the dumpster could be the difference of no trash pick-up for two or three extra days. Over a month, this could save you $200 to $300. The list of controllables is seemingly endless. Noncontrollables are easy to put into the budget. For the most part, they will not change from month to month. An example of a noncontrollable item would be the restaurants rent or lease.Sometimes the restaurant's rent or lease will be based on a percentage of the total revenue for that period and sometimes it will be a fixed cost for a 4- or 5-week period based on the square footage of your restaurant. As you can see in 2.5, I have put a lease with the percentage of the lease (under building rent) being only 1.78%. Therefore, according to this budget, if you budget the total revenue at $265,000, then the lease for the month would be $4,725 (265,000 × .0178 = 4725.00). Remember: to find ways to cut back on the budget in certain areas in order to save money, you may not be able to find it in your noncontrollables. If you are running a chain restaurant, this will depend on what your corporate definition of what is or is not a noncontrollable. For example, say the corporate office defines your alarm and monitoring company as a noncontrollable. It is a constant cost that will not change from month to month. However, simply because something is a noncontrollable does not mean it is the best price and lowest cost that can be found for your budget. You could shop around and find a better price with a company that is just as good. Therefore, in a way, a manager could control a noncontrollable. The reason they are called noncontrollables is that, for the most part, a manager cannot control them. No matter how much revenue you generate or do not generate during a given period or how much you would like to decrease the money you are spending on them, it is not possible to do so. This goes back to the example of your car payment. You can change the monthly payment by driving a different car that is just as reliable, but once you have chosen a car, it is more difficult to change the monthly payments.

Now you have a complete budget and an idea of what numbers you need to hit. All you have to do is sit back and let the restaurant run itself, right? Wrong!

Getting back to my wife's and my budget, we felt the same way. We wrote a budget for ourselves and looked at it at the end of the month to see where we were. We found we were better off than before, but we were still broke and not saving a dime in our savings account. Again, I went to those who knew best: our parents. They made me realize that by creating a budget I was just taking the first step to controlling our money. All a budget does for me is make me aware of upcoming expenses and where I stand at the beginning of the month. In no way does a budget tell me where I will end up at the end of the month. Therefore, I decided I needed to add a few things to my budget— something that would assure me that on a day-to-day basis I could look at my checkbook, compare it to my budget, and with a little addition and subtraction, I would know exactly where I was. Here is a look at the budget I created.

2.6 My Personal Budget

July '03

Account Balance:	$274.00
My checks:	$2,500.00
Her checks:	$2,397.30
Total earns:	**$5,171.30**

BILLS	BUDGET	ACTUAL
Mortgage	$1,398.00	$1,398.00
Car 1	$366.22	$366.22
Car 2	$341.74	$341.74
Cell Phones	$101.00	$101.00
Telephone	$80.00	$80.00
Electric Bill	$185.00	$185.00
Gas Bill	$65.00	$65.00
Insurance	$199.98	$199.98
Visa	$100.00	$100.00
Discover	$100.00	$100.00
Amex	$250.00	$250.00
Mastercard	$150.00	$150.00
Internet	$28.00	$28.00
Groceries	$300.00	$300.00
Entertainment	$310.00	$310.00
Dry Cleaners	$35.00	$35.00
Lunch Money	$110.00	$110.00
Gas for Cars	$90.00	$90.00
Hair Cuts	$40.00	$40.00
Special Events:	$100.00	$100.00
Vitamins:	$75.00	$75.00
Total Expenses:	**$4,424.94**	**$4,424.94**

We have:	$5,171.30
We owe:	$4,424.94
Savings:	$746.36
Bottom line:	**$746.36**

Savings:	**$1,674.36**

Date	Amount	For What

Date	Amount	For What

As you can see in 2.6, I have detailed all our personal debts on a piece of paper and called it a budget. As I said before, I really wanted to know where we were going to stand at the beginning of the month, at the middle of the month, and at the end of the month.

To start off my budget, I wanted to know how much money we were starting out with in the bank and add this to the checks that my wife and I would receive that month. This gave me the total income (total revenue). Then I had to list all of our expenses.

In order for me to see where we were each day, I inserted spaces where I could put down any money that we spent on a daily basis. Anytime we got gas, went to the cleaners, went out to eat (even buying a coke at a quick stop), or bought groceries we wrote it in the space provided. This assured me that we were staying within my budget. Sometimes, however, if we went over the allotted amount in a certain category, we would have to cut back in other areas of the budget in order to make up for it. Another area that we used on a day-to-day basis was the bottom portion of the budget for entertainment. Entertainment covers everything from buying a stick of gum, putting a quarter in the meter, buying fast food, or eating out and catching a movie. My wife and I include everything that is not listed on the budget into entertainment. This also includes clothes, new furniture, and so forth. Now, if we know in advance that we are going to spend money on clothes or furniture or anything else outside of entertainment, we add it to the list of expenses. As shown in 2.6 in the entertainment section, we have budgeted $10 a day, $70 a week (for the month of July $310, since July has 31 days in it). Each day we write down the total amount we spent in entertainment in the space provided. At the end of the week, we tally the week's total expenditure and see where we stand. If we have gone over, then we cut back the next week or cut back in another area. If we are under our budget, then we try to put more toward savings.

This process of keeping track of a particular item on a day-to-day basis and watching the expenses closely for any rise or fall in a given month can be summed up in two words—declining budget!

Chapter Three:

"I think our real problem is the damn graphs."

The Declining Budget

A budget is good to have, but it should not end there. Just as my wife and I found out when we completed our personal budget, all a budget can do is give you a place to begin and indicate to you where you could end up. In order for a budget to work in a restaurant, you must watch over each individual department from the very beginning of the period, ensuring they are all on track, with the sales numbers that have been budgeted reflecting those that have been generated. An easy way to stay on top of it all is by using a declining budget. That way you can determine where you will end up by crunching the numbers throughout the period. A declining budget might sound difficult to manage, but most of us have a head start on how to maintain a declining budget without even knowing it.

A declining budget is just like keeping a checkbook. Yes, it is just that simple. Think about it. You start out your checkbook with a certain dollar amount and then you pay all your bills according to how much money is in the account at the time they are due. This is done without ever going over what you started out with. Timing is essential to both a checkbook and a declining budget. If you write a check for $500 when your account has $350 in it, you will end up bouncing a check. It is the same in the restaurant industry. If you bounce a check to the produce company because you did not manage your declining budget correctly, then the company may stop doing business with you and your credit report will reflect poor scores. Oh yes, just as in your personal life, bouncing a check in the restaurant industry will cause your restaurant to suffer some serious negative consequences. This is just another reason why it is important to maintain a declining budget and refrain from writing bad checks. Now, if you cannot keep a checkbook correctly, then you may have a little difficulty handling a declining budget. All you need to do is maintain your declining budget on a daily basis. How is this done? Well, take a look at a declining budget up close and see if you can figure out why you actually need one.

3.1 Declining Budget

DECLINING BUDGET

Budgeted Sales for the Month of July: **$265,000.00**
Budgeted Dollars to Spend for the Month: **$2,200.00**
Budgeted Percentage to Spend for the Month: **0.83%**

LAUNDRY AND UNIFORMS

Day of Month	Amount of Invoice	Month to Date Total	Left to Spend	% per Day	% for Month
1	$78.89	$78.89	$2,121.11	0.03%	0.03%
2	$105.05	$183.94	$2,016.06	0.04%	0.07%
3	$0.00	$183.94	$2,016.06	0.00%	0.07%
4	$209.76	$393.70	$1,806.30	0.08%	0.15%
5					
6					
7					
8					
9					
10					
11					
12					
13					
14					
15					
16					
17					
18					
19					
20					
21					
22					
23					
24					
25					
26					
27					
28					
29					
30					
31					

This is just one example of a declining budget; there are other ways of keeping a declining budget.

The key to a declining budget is to always update it with current information. A couple of ways to ensure that the budget is being updated, follow these two steps:

- Keep a log for each department's budget and declining budget where they are easy to get at and where current numbers can be found (e.g., the manager's office, general manager's office, or controller's office).

- Have the declining budgets enlarged and laminated and post them on the wall outside the manager's office so everyone can see where they are on a daily basis (dry-erase markers work well for this).

In looking at 3.1, you can see that this declining budget is for laundry and uniforms in the month of July. In order for you to fill in the blanks for total revenue, percent, and budgeted dollar amount, you need to return to the budget on 2.1 (The Budget). Your budget shows that you plan to have a total revenue of $265,000 and you need your laundry and uniform to stay at .83%, or $2,200 for the period (see "laundry and uniform" in column two of 2.1 for these numbers). Now that you have your numbers, you can plug them in at the top of the declining budget where there are blanks provided. You are now ready to start a declining budget for the month.

I have chosen to do the first four days to give an idea of how the declining budget works. As you can see in column one of the declining budget, I have simply put the day. This should always correlate with the actual day of the month you are on. If there is a day you do not spend anything, then you need to indicate that by entering "$0" in the space provided and calculate all the other columns (as I have done on day three). The second column is the total dollar amount spent for that day in that particular department. This means that any money paid out or any invoices signed off on for that day are added together and the total goes in the space. The third column adds the total daily amounts spent. Once you have the total amount spent for the month to date, you then subtract this amount from your budgeted amount, and this is what makes up column four. The fifth column is optional. It is for tracking the daily percentage.

This can be done by taking the budgeted dollar amount at the top of the page, subtracting it by the daily amount, then taking the total and dividing it by the total revenue.

2,200.00 (budgeted amount to spend in this category)
−   78.89 (daily amount spent)
2,121.11 ———   2,121.11
÷ 265,000.00 (total revenue)
.03 (daily percentage used)

This is optional because it does not let you know where you are headed in terms of the budget. All it tells you is that, for that day and that day only, you ended the day with that percentage. The reason I like it on the declining budget is that it makes it easier to see any discrepancies. If I want my spending to be consistent all period long, or if I want to alert myself when my spending is too high, this column provides me with a quick reference. As you can see on day one, 0.03% of the total revenue was spent, and on the fourth day, 0.08% was spent. It is now possible to go back and find out why so much was spent on that particular day. Maybe there was a banquet. Perhaps it was a Friday, so the restaurant had to get ready for the weekend, and day one is a Monday when it is slow enough that you only need half the laundry and uniforms. One of the reasons to use a declining budget is for situations like these. When they arise, you can prevent problems before they happen, or you can adjust either your budget (to take away from some other department) or your spending in an area for the rest of the month. The sixth column is similar to the fifth, with one exception. The sixth column increases the percentage with every dollar spent in the department. This column lets you know how close you are to your budgeted percentage. If you have already used up 0.15% of your 0.83% budgeted in four days, then you need to slow down the spending in this department or adjust the budget.

Remember, if your sales are not reaching your budget, then you need to adjust your declining budgets revenue and dollar amounts in all departments. The only time you should have to change the percentage is when you are at your break point for any category.

Also, remember that this is just one way to do a declining budget for any given department. Some departments have to be viewed on a much larger scale with more than just percentages involved. For example, labor is one of the most difficult percentages to control.

Chapter Four:

"What do I think is the strongest feature of my resume? Well, definitely the fact that none of it can be checked."

Labor Control

Labor consists of those persons who are paid by their employer for services rendered. This includes office personnel, servers, bartenders, kitchen employees, management, and so forth. The reason labor can be so difficult to manage is due to the amount of people who are involved. How many times have you heard another employee say, "I forgot to clock out," "I didn't punch in when I got here," "I punched in early because I was already here," or maybe, "I can't work on Sunday," or a manager who says, "I needed a couple of extra bodies to get us through the rush, so I called in some more employees"? These are just a few of the many ways in which labor can be altered on a daily basis. Now, do not get me wrong; by no means is labor supposed to be a number set in stone. Unfortunately, things happen over which you have no control. People get sick, relatives pass away, people are injured, some are let go due to performance or some other problems, some go on vacations, others move on to "real jobs," and all of these have an effect on your labor percentage as well. Labor is all about numbers and percentages.

Remember early on when I said numbers do not lie? Well, when you get into looking at labor percentages you will see how important that statement is. In order to start looking at labor you must first understand—even with all the externals that can affect labor—it can be controlled, as long as it is managed properly. How? Well, look at it this way. When people go to sleep and need to be at work the next morning, most set an alarm clock to wake them. Now, this alarm is set to go off at a certain time. This time is usually chosen on the notion that we are giving ourselves enough time to wake up, get ready for work, and be at work on time, right? This is called time management. *Time management* is the ability to finish all of a task needing to be done in or before the time frame allotted. For this example, say a person allows herself one hour to wake up and to get to work on time. This means, if she manages her time (time management) correctly, she should be able to finish showering, brush her teeth, get dressed, and everything else (including driving) in order to make it to work on time in one hour. There are even those times when she likes to get that extra sleep and push it a little more by hitting the snooze button a couple of times. Her incentive, of course, is to get extra sleep and, in return, she has to manage her time a little better by having to get to work in a shorter period of time. For those of us who do hit the snooze button, we always seem to find a way.

You are probably saying, "That's great to hear about time management in the morning, but what does that have to do with restaurant labor?" Well, time management is the whole basis for labor. You see, before going straight to a piece of paper and crunching hours for an employee schedule, it is important to know what it takes to do the job of the employees that you are scheduling. How else are you going to know when to schedule people and when not to? For example, say we were doing the kitchen schedule. How would I know how many prep cooks I would need on any given day? I would have to know each position well enough to know how long it takes to actually prep each item. Why do you think, when you are going through a management training program in the kitchen, the training has you peeling 400 pounds of shrimp, or you have to make 120 pieces of the same item? It is not because the program believes it actually takes the average person 120 tries before they understand and can correctly do the process. It has to make you understand the way the employee feels and how long it may take to actually complete the prep on that particular item. After peeling 200 pounds of shrimp, the employee becomes bored and tired. This means that the first 200 pounds might only take an hour, where the next 200 may take him two hours, for a total of three hours to complete the prep. Once we have learned this we can then apply some time management and find some ways in which we can improve our labor. Let us say that the person peeling the shrimp is being paid $6.50 an hour. If he were to peel 400 pounds of shrimp, it would take him three hours to complete the prep, and would therefore cost $19.50. If we know this, we can schedule another employee, who is making $6.50 an hour, and have him doing the prep as well. Remember, we found that one employee could do 200 pounds in one hour and 400 pounds in three hours. Now that we have two employees working on the prep, we can get 400 pounds of shrimp peeled in two hours and it would only cost us $13.00. Although we added an extra body on the schedule, we were able to shave an hour off prep and were able to save $6.50. Another way to cut even more cost is by giving the two employees incentives. As we do with ourselves in the snooze-alarm theory, you may find that what may have taken an hour before takes less time when you give people incentives.

Another thing to analyze before making your schedule is the strengths of your employees and the positions for which you are scheduling them. When going through your departments, whether it's servers, bussers, or line cooks, you need to have your key players in place. Before you can do this, you must know what your highest strength positions are. Highest strength positions are simply the places in the schedule—whether it's a certain station on the floor, a certain time frame that the hostess/host stand will be slammed, or a position on the kitchen line—that you need to schedule someone on whom you can depend and that you know will get the job done. These people you select to put in the highest strength positions are more than likely going to be your highest-paid people. Since they are your highest-paid employees, you need to make sure you balance out the schedule on those particular shifts so you do not go over your budget. For example, say you are scheduling a Friday night for the kitchen line. You know you are going to be extremely busy from 6:00 PM to 10:00 PM. Now, you can figure out different ways that you can schedule people so everyone is a winner. You never want to schedule your highest-dollar laborers for long or short hours. If you schedule them for long hours, they could hit overtime and you may miss your budget. If you schedule them for short hours, then you are not being fair to them and, more than likely, they will let you know by either performing poorly or quitting.

Even though you are crunching numbers and trying to meet your budget to make your profit line, you need to remember those employees who are helping you get the results. How would you like it if you were an hourly making $10 an hour and working only thirty hours a week, and then you receive a promotion, which made you salaried, paying you $500 a week, but you had to start working sixty hours a

week? That is not a promotion. That is highway robbery. By attempt-
ing to do this to an employee you are making them work twice the
hours with less than twice the pay. Your employees are the ones keeping you in business, so make them happy and, in return, they will
perform better. If you are cheap with your employees so you can hit a
better percentage, you will find that you will not be in business long. I
am not saying you ought pay your employees all $10 an hour, but I am
saying you ought not pay them all minimum wage.

Once you have figured this out, you can even use it to your advan-
tage. In the restaurant business it is sometimes difficult to get people
to work on Sundays. For some restaurants, other shifts are hard to get
employees to work as well. When you give out raises, you ought to
inform the employee that along with the raise comes more responsibility, and that they need to be able to work the days and shifts that
you need them to work. When I say more responsibility, I am talking
about the ways in which you can coordinate the schedule. For example,
you are scheduling for the line cooks on Monday night. You schedule
four people on the line (they make $6.00, $7.00, $7.50, and $8.00 an
hour), or if the person who is making $10.00 an hour is as good as his
pay says he is, you might then be able to schedule only three people
(making $6.00, $8.00 and $10.00 an hour), and save $4.50 per hour
in labor. This also gives you the chance to use the $7.00 and $7.50
employees on other days without them going into overtime.

Now, there are many other ways to play with the schedule so that
everyone is in a win-win situation, but you do not necessarily need to
use a particular person all the time. I have just shown you a few examples to get your mind working in the direction of crunching numbers.
Also, remember your break points. If you do not remember what this
is, then you need to go back and read the first chapter again.

Scheduling is usually done by breaking the employees into the
departments that coordinate with the budget. Making a schedule is
quite simple. The only difficult part is trying to ensure you are hitting
your budgeted numbers. A big key when making a schedule against a
budget is to make the schedule fall below the budget. Make sure you

schedule fewer employees/hours so you are spending fewer dollars on your schedule than what your budget actually has for that particular department. This is referred to as padding the schedule for budget purposes. This will allow you to use more labor, if needed, during the week than originally planned. If you make your schedule to match what the budget is projecting, then you are not taking into consideration all the outside elements that can affect the outcome of your labor percentage. Remember, employees sometimes clock in early or clock out late, managers ask employees to stay longer, or even ask some that were not on the schedule to come in and help out. Any variations from what you have on your schedule will obviously change your labor percentage.

Another item that can change your labor percentage is sales. When making your budget and your schedule, you have given the revenue that you assume you will hit. In the restaurant business, sales can be anything but steady. They can be one of the most difficult things to predict, not to mention the fact that most budgets are written a year in advance. If for some reason your revenue has had an unexpected decline during the week, then, just as you would adjust your budget and declining budgets, you need to adjust your schedules. There are two easy ways to do this. One way is by cutting sections early or bringing employees in certain sections in at later times. The next way would be to simply call off certain stations. If you do not see the need for ten employees, then call the ones you can do without and ask them not to come in for that shift. A simple call to the employee prior to them coming in may be all you need, and it is certainly better than alienating them by asking them if they want to be off after they have driven all the way to work. The employees that you call will appreciate not having to drive to work just to get sent home because the revenue is not high enough. In some states it is the law that if an employee shows up for work as scheduled, you have to pay them for a full two hours of work, whether they are sent home after twenty minutes or not. So asking an employee to volunteer is a safe way to lessen the amount of employees on a shift.

Now you need to take a look at a schedule and find out how to figure the cost and percentages to meet the needs of your budget. Looking at the kitchen department, you can get a feel for how different pay rates affect the numbers. Schedules can be made in any way you choose to. Whether you want your schedule to look professional by printing it, or whether you just want to handwrite it is up to you. There are even some computer labor programs that you can download onto a computer that will do most of the number crunching for you. All you have to do is enter all of the employees' information and how many hours you would like to schedule them, and the computer does the rest. Some labor software on the market is for small businesses only, so be sure to do your homework on the many programs available if this is the route you choose to take.

4.1 The Schedule

	THURSDAY 3/16 (CL = 11)		FRIDAY 3/17 (CL = 12)		SATURDAY 3/22 (CL = 12)		SUNDAY 3/19 (CL = 11)		MONDAY 3/20 (CL = 11)		TUESDAY 3/21 (CL = 11)		WEDNESDAY 3/22 (CL = 11)	
	L	D	L	D	L	D	L	D	L	D	L	D	L	D
Lunch														
Name 1	8.3//broil				8.3//sau								8.3//pb	
Name 2			8.3-3pb	5-10pr	8.3-3pb		8.3//pa				9-3pb			
Name 3	8.3//sau		8.3//sau				8.3//sau				8.3//sau		8.3//sau	
Name 4	7.3//prtrk		8.3//ps		8.3//pz		Happy Birthday		8.3//ps		9//pr			
Name 5	8.3//ps				8.3//sal		8.3//pz		8.3//st		8.3//ps			
Name 6	8.3//trpb		8.3//trpb				8.3//br		8.3//pb					
Name 7			8//pr		9//pr		9//pr		10pr				9//pr	
Dinner														
Name 1		5//pr				4-10.3pr	5-10pr					5//sal		5//sal
Name 2				5//br		5//br		5//br		4//pb		4//pb		
Name 3		6-10//sal		4//sau		4//sau						4//sau		6-10//sal
Name 4				5//sau		5//sau			8.3//sau	4//sau		8.3//ps		
Name 5		4//pb		4.3//pa		4//pa		4//pa						4//pb
Name 6		5//pz		5//pz				5//pz		5//pz				
Name 7				6-10.3sal		6//pz						6//pz		6//pz
Name 8					8.3//trsell			4//trbld		5//trbld		5//trbld		5//trbld
Name 9		4//sau		server	server	server		4//sau						4//sau
Dish														
Name 1		5-9sal			10//st	5//sal	8.3//sal	5-10//sal	5//sal					
Name 2	10//st		10//st					10//st			10//st		10//st	
Name 3		4//trst		5//st				4//st				5//st		
Name 4		6//st		6//st	6//st									6//st
Busser														
Name 1				5//bus		5//bus		4//bus	9//bus					5//bus
Name 2	9//bus		9//bus		9//bus		9//bus				9//bus		9//bus	
Name 3		5//bus		5//bus		5//bus			5//bus		5//bus			

As shown in 4.1, I will first talk about a schedule that has been made for the kitchen without any dollars and percentages. At the top of the schedule, you see the days and dates are posted. Although this seems elementary, I have seen a few managers post a schedule without one or the other. Why should you have to post both the date and the day? Well, take a closer look at the schedule, and you will see the dates I have on this schedule are out of order. Therefore, it makes it possible for the employee to see what I meant to do, and they will still show up for their scheduled shift. In my experience, employees are notorious for suddenly being unable to read a schedule and or misread the time they are due to arrive. Right under the dates you see a CL = 11 or a CL = 12. I have put this on the schedule to indicate the time I want my employees to clock out if they are the ones closing that night (CL means close). Putting the out times on the posted schedule is optional. Sometimes, if you put the time out, your employees might become dependent on it. When the restaurant is slow, you always get the employees out before their time out posted. When you become busy on an unexpected shift and try to keep your employees on after their posted time, you may find your employees have already told their other job or family they would be able to be there at a certain time. Either way, you still need to have your out times posted for your management team. The best way I have found that you can maintain your budget is by allowing the managers to know when you expect your staff in and when you expect your staff to leave.

The last step before making the schedule is to separate the different stations. If you are running an existing restaurant, you may not need to break out the categories if most of your employees in the kitchen are cross-trained (cross-trained refers to those employees who can work various stations). I usually set categories on the schedule when I am opening a restaurant and work toward no categories within four to six months after opening. For this schedule, I have separated my day employees from my night ones. I have done so by naming and separating the column and implementing an employee in all the times that are needed in order to hit my break points. Separating the employees by lunch and dinner is optional. Again, I work toward not having to do this by cross-training my employees. This benefits me in the situations I get in when I have a cook who gets sick and cannot show for work. I have more options to get the employee's shift covered than if I had not cross-trained my employees.

Now you are ready to schedule your employees. Remember all the things that have been discussed while you are making out your schedule.

Here is a brief list of the things you need to take into consideration before you start to write a schedule:

1) Break points

2) Know the revenue budgeted for that day

3) Know the strength of positions

4) Know the strengths of the employees

5) Pad your schedule for budgeting purposes

These are done in the order that I make out my schedules. To tell you the truth, it has worked for me for years. Before I even start making a schedule, I figure out what my basic need is for each day in those stations (break points). In order to do this I must know the revenue I have budgeted for the day. There is a huge difference when you are scheduling prep or any department's position for a day if you are looking to do $4,000 in revenue as opposed to a day on which your expected revenue is $17,000. After I have these two in mind, I look down my schedule to find the positions that are going to need someone I can depend on to get the job done. Once I've located those positions and have the first two steps in mind, I then plug in my strongest employees. After I have them on the schedule, I can then go back and fill in the rest of the positions with weaker employees. While I am doing this, I am still considering the strength of the employee and the strength of the position. When I have my schedule completely filled out the way I want it, I then go back and crunch numbers to see if the schedule falls between my budgeted dollar and percentage amounts for kitchen labor. After determining whether it has fallen below or above the budget, I can then go back and make the necessary adjustments.

If you are lucky enough to get long-term, stable employees in the front of the house or the back of the house, I would suggest doing a set schedule. Set a solid schedule for each semester of school if you have student employees. If you do it for the servers, you will not have to worry about shifts that come up that the employees would rather not work. For your staff, it gives them a stable environment that does not keep them guessing. If they have an exam coming, they know they need to get their shift covered so they can study. Moreover, if any of your employees are going out of town, they already know when they work and need to get shifts covered. The last thing I will mention about set schedules is the relief it gives you. I am sure you have plenty of things you need to take care of during the week and would like it if you did not have to produce a new schedule every week.

Now extend your schedule so you can see how you get your dollars and percentages. This will give you the information you need so you can relate it to the budget. There are many ways a schedule can look and be done. I have just given you this as an example so you can find out how to crunch numbers from a schedule.

4.2 The Performa

	THURSDAY 3/16		FRIDAY 3/17		SATURDAY 3/22		SUNDAY 3/19		MONDAY 3/20		TUESDAY 3/21		WEDNESDAY 3/22		HRS	PAY	TP
	CL = 11		CL = 12		CL = 12		CL = 11		CL = 11		CL = 11		CL = 11				
Lunch	L	D	L	D	L	D	L	D	L	D	L	D	L	D			
Name 1	8.3//broil				8.3//sau						8.3//pb				18	$11.00	$178.00
Name 2			8.3-3pb	5-10pr	8.3-3pb		8.3//pa				9-3pb				31.5	$9.50	$299.25
Name 3	8.3//sau		8.3//sau				8.3//sau				8.3//sau		8.3//sau		35.5	$10.75	$381.63
Name 4	7.3//prtrk		8.3//ps		8.3//pz		Happy Birthday		8.3//ps		9//pr				41	$8.75	$342.38
Name 5	8.3//ps				8.3//sal		8.3//pz		8.3//st		8.3//ps						
Name 6	8.3//trpb		8.3//trpb				8.3//br		8.3//pb								
Name 7			8//pr		9//pr		9//pr		10pr				9//pr		31	$8.50	$261.56
Dinner																	
Name 1		5//pr				4-10.3pr		5-10pr				5//sal		5//sal			
Name 2				5//br		5//br		5//br		4//pb		4//pb					
Name 3		6-10//sal		4//sau		4//sau						4//sau		6-10//sal	38	$11.00	$805.00
Name 4				5//sau		5//sau				8.3//sau	4//sau			8.3//ps	35.75	$8.25	$284.94
Name 5		4//pb		4.3//pa		4//pa		4//pa						4//pb	35	$9.25	$323.75
Name 6		5//pa		5//pa				5//pa		5//pa					24.25	$7.50	$181.88
Name 7				6-10.3sal		6//pz						6//pz		6//pz	21.25	$7.50	$159.38
Name 8					8.3//trsell		4//trbld		5//trbld		5//trbld		5//trbld		27	$9.00	$238.00
Name 9		4//sau		server		server		server	4//sau					4//sau	19.25	$8.50	$163.63
Dish																	
Name 1		5-9sal				10//st	5//sal	8.3//sal	5-10//sal		5//sal				32.5	$7.50	$243.75
Name 2	10//st		10//st				10//st				10//st		10//st		34.5	$7.30	$241.50
Name 3			4//trst		5//st				4//st				5//st		0	$7.00	$0.00
Name 4			6//st		6//st		6//st							6//st	40	$7.00	$280.00
															459.5		$3,890.58
													Avrg Hrly Rate				$8.47
													$40,000.00				9.73%
													$45,000.00				8.65%
													$35,000.00				11.17%

The Performa is when you extend out your schedule to include your cost of having that labor scheduled for that period of time. As you can see in 4.2, all I have done is added an extra three columns. The first column, HRS, stands for hours. This indicates the amount of hours that a particular employee is scheduled to work for that week. This can be calculated by adding up the amount of hours the employee is working each day. The second column, PAY, stands for the employee's hourly rate of pay. The third column, TP, stands for the total pay in dollars that will be paid to that particular employee if the hours that are indicated on the schedule are completed at the end of the week. This can be calculated by simply taking one employee's hours in the HRS column and multiplying it by the employees rate found in the PAY column (e.g., John has 30 hours and is paid $9 an hour, so you take $30 \times 9 = 270$). Once you have done this for every employee and you have your columns full all the way down, you are ready to move to the next step.

Now you need to add each employee's hours to the other employees' hours all the way down the column. Do the same for the third column. You will get a total for hours, and pay at the bottom of the schedule. I have already done this for you in the example. Now you have a total for each column and can move on to the final step before comparing it with the budget.

At the bottom of 4.2, you can see that the total wages are $3,890.56. This is the number you want to compare to the budget to make sure it's within the budgeted dollar amount.

Before doing this, you need to find out your percentage. To find the labor percentage for the kitchen, take the total pay and divide it by the budgeted food revenue for this particular week. To find the labor percentage for any other labor department you must take the total wages and divide them by the total revenue for this particular week. The reason restaurants use only the food revenue to find the kitchen percentage is because this is the only thing for which the kitchen is responsible. Not all restaurants do it this way, but most of the ones in my experience do. All other departments have a toll on the total revenue, and therefore you must use the total revenue to find their percentages. The only exception I have seen to this rule is the bar. Some companies use the budgeted bar revenue to figure out the bartenders labor percentage. Either way is okay, as long as you use it consistently.

Let's say that, for this example, you budgeted $40,000.00 in food revenue for this particular week. Knowing this, you can then take our total wages of $3,890.56, divide it by your budgeted food revenue of $40,000.00, and find that you have scheduled a labor percentage of 9.73%.

3890.56 (total wages for the week)

÷ 40000.00 (food revenue for the week)

0.0973 (labor percentage for the week)

Now refer back to the budget in 2.4. Here you find the budgeted kitchen staff labor is at 10%. This means that the current schedule is just barely falling below the budget. If you feel confident that no one will alter the scheduled hours in any way, then you can post the schedule. If you feel that you did not pad it enough, then you ought to go back and adjust the schedule accordingly.

Along with dollars and percentages that deal directly with the budget, many companies like to look at something called productivity that does not even show up on the budget, but it helps get an idea of what is happening in the labor department. *Productivity* deals directly with the management involvement both in making the schedule and while on the shift. Productivity tells, on an hourly basis, what dollar amount each employee has contributed. In other words, I am saying that, in the first hour of business, you did $1000 and had ten servers on at that time, then they each contributed $100 for the first hour of business. Obviously, the higher the dollar amount, the more productive the employees are.

The reason some companies like to look at this more so than the percentages, is because this number holds relatively steady in comparison to the percentages and the result is due to total management involvement. Although you may be running a shift for which someone else has made the schedule, you have total control over keeping and cutting your employees. This is simply saying that, if you were to look at productivity instead of percentages for a particular shift, then all that matters is how long you kept your employees on the clock. It does not matter who was on the clock and how much they were making. Productivity simply takes the total revenue and divides it by the total labor hours in a particular department in a particular day. Once again, the same rule applies for the kitchen as when determining a kitchen labor percentage; you only use the food revenue. Say that your total revenue for one day was $12,500.00 and your server hours added up to 140. You would then take your total revenue of $12,500.00 and divide this by your server hours of 140 and we would get an end result of $89.29.

> 12,500 (total daily revenue)
> ÷   140 (total server hours)
>   89.29 (productivity in dollar amounts)

The closer the number is to $90.00 (or higher), the better. If you go too far over $90.00, then you may be cheating the guest out of a better experience because you have too few servers on. If you fall way below $75.00, then you may have too many servers on, and you are not cutting your servers when the restaurant slows down. The good thing about productivity is that you can find out how you are doing just by knowing your department hours for the day and the total revenue for the day. This makes for an easy way to double-check your standing. The bad thing about productivity is that it does not tell you on whom those hours are being spent. You could have 140 hours of employees being paid $6.00 an hour or $12.00 an hour and it would still give you the productivity of $89.29. This is why, when you look at or talk about the budget or P&L, you do it with currency and percentage. Numbers do not lie. Another place you can see just how important currency and percentages is in the biggest area that affects your restaurant, and yet it can be as difficult to manage as labor: cost of sales.

Chapter Five:

Cost of Sales

Remember, *cost of sales* refers to the amount of money and percent of revenue it cost, in consumables, in order to create the revenue. You have to buy the consumables, so you may in turn sell them to your customers. All categories within c.o.s. have only to do with consumables items that will be purchased by the guest. Costs of sales are broken down into selected categories so the profit and loss may be easily tracked. This way, a manager will know where to look if costs get out of line. The categories are as follows: food, beverage, liquor, beer, and wine. Food is then broken into subcategories. These categories depend on the type of restaurant for which you are budgeting. Subcatagories under food for example could be: dairy, seafood, crab, shrimp, groceries, bakery, and produce.

Before looking into how you get your cost of sales, you need to start from the beginning. First, you need to get the consumables into the restaurant. The moves that are made from the beginning will determine the outcome of your cost.

Buying your product from vendors can sometimes seem very easy. What is so hard about picking up the phone, giving your order to someone, and waiting for the order to arrive? Well, as easy as that sounds, there is much more to the overall picture than most realize. How can you give an order to anyone if you are not sure what you need?

Every restaurant, big or small, needs to develop order sheets for any product they plan to order and receive. Order sheets make it easier to see what you have on hand and what you will need to order. They also show you the quantity in which you need to order.

5.1 Order Sheet

Produce Order Sheet

Contact Name: Carole Zapoli   Phone: (713) 455-1616

Weekly Sales:_____

Item	Unit Size	Cost Per Unit	Mon&Wed Par	Mon 22-Aug		Wed 24-Aug		Fri Par	Fri 26-Aug	
				OH	OR	OH	OR		OH	OR
Yellow Onion	50# sack	17.5	7					11		
Red Onion	50# sack	14.65	3					6		
Bananas	10# cs	8.99	20#					40#		
Tomatoes	5x6 cs	21.35	12					18		
Avacado	Haas #2cs	27.85	10					18		
Red Bells	Medium/cs	31.56	2					4		
Green Bells	Medium/cs	24.22	2					4		
Limes	200ct/cs	26.52	2					4		
Oranges	88ct/cs	18.59	2					4		
Lemons	200ct/cs	20.78	2					4		

As you can see in 5.1, order sheets should give you the product name, the product number (if the item does not have a product number, then use the size, count, or weight, especially when ordering produce), the par level with unit size (examples of unit size are: each, case, bottle, container, pound, etc.), a column for what you have in inventory (OH = on hand), how much you need to order (OR = order) and the price at which you are ordering it. Note that the vendor is at the top of the page with the phone number and the representative to call.

In order to create a sheet like this you must establish your par levels for all the items you plan to order. If you are opening a store and do not currently have a par set for each item, it is suggested that you order a little heavy on your initial order. There is nothing worse than having a customer wanting to give you money in exchange for something you are out of because you did not buy enough of that particular item. After making your first two orders, you can then set your pars. The way in which to set par levels is simple. You take what you had on hand from last time and subtract from it what you have on hand when you do your count. Let us say you ordered five cases of tomatoes last time and when you go to do your order, you have only two cases left.

This means the restaurant used three cases from the last order to this order. Par levels are never set in stone and fluctuate with the revenue and times of the year. If the restaurant used three cases of tomatoes, it is wise to set your par level at four or five cases so you have extra in case the revenue suddenly increases during the week. If you order the same thing twice in one week, it is smart to create two different par levels, as I have done in 5.1. In this example, I plan to order produce three times a week. I have two separate pars, one for Monday and Wednesday, and one for Friday.

Now that you have what you need, you can make a call and place your order, right? In most cases, this is correct. If your restaurant is part of a big company, then most likely they will have a few contracts set up with certain vendors that you are required to use. Companies do this in order to receive big discounts. In addition, certain vendors usually control particular brands of liquor, beer, and wine. When it comes to produce, meats, and seafood, most restaurants are not under any contracts. The reasons companies do not like to set contracts in these areas are the ever-changing price and the competition among vendors.

For example, produce prices are up and down throughout the year. One week lettuce is at $8.90 a case, and the next week it is at $24.00 a case. When you factor in competition, you have your own little stock market going. You need to know when to buy, when to buy in quantity, and when to let go of a particular vendor and buy from someone else. When choosing between vendors, remember that price is not the only thing with which to be concerned. It is amazing how some vendors try to get your business. Some may try to sell you the same product for $10.00 cheaper than their next competitor. Although this sounds great, you need to investigate further. Maybe you are being sold a product that the vendor is just trying to get rid of because it is of poor quality. Some produce companies will beat all the prices of the company you are currently dealing with. Your first reaction might be to question your current vendor's pricing. Remember, you must always investigate. Go to the company's facility and look at how they run their operation. Sometimes this is all it takes. You may be amazed at how many produce plants have open boxes lying around, dirty floors, or poor-quality cooling. Some could even have rats running around! While you are there, take a look at their delivery trucks.

I once had a kitchen manager who told me he visited a company's facility and everything was a go. When the day came for them to deliver our produce, I was excited to see how this company's produce compared to our current vendor's. When the produce arrived (finally, at 5:00 PM when we normally get our deliveries at 9:00 AM), it was delivered in the back of a pickup truck. I was told that they only had two trucks with refrigeration and they were being used for other customers. I was also told that the rest of my order would be out later that night because my order could not fit in the back of the truck.

Touring a company's facility will open your eyes in so many ways. Once you have looked at the facility, you need to consider the delivery dates and times. Things you need to consider here include how many days a week will you need to order and what the best time for you to receive the order will be for you to have sufficient time to check it in. The number of days a week you will receive your orders can depend on the amount of storage space you have and how many items are cooked fresh daily. If you have plenty of space, I would set deliveries as few times a week as possible. There are so many things that you need to control, instead of spending your time inventorying, ordering, checking in, and putting away product six days a week. The time to receive your product is quite simple: before or after lunch. As simplistic as this may sound, if you do not inform your purveyors as to the time you would like the delivery to hit your back door, they will show up in the middle of lunch or after all of your prep people have gone home. In my experience, the best time for delivery is between 8:00 AM and 11:00 AM. This way you can send back an item that is not up to your specs and still get the right item delivered to you the same day. These times will also help you if you need something for lunch and you are out of that particular item, so it will be coming in on the truck.

When placing your order, make sure you are very descriptive. If you want to order salmon, you would need to specify the way you would like to receive it. You could get the salmon whole, a side, portioned, or IQF (individually quick-frozen). If it is a side of salmon you want, you then need to specify how many pounds and whether you want it boneless, skinless, or something else. If you want the salmon to be portioned, then you need to specify whether you want a filet cut or a steak cut. With anything you order, make sure you have the correct specifications. If you are unsure of the specs you need, ask someone who knows within your company or look it up in your company spec books. If you're out on your own, or you are getting this item in for the first time, and you are not sure what you want, ask your representative for help. Your rep can even bring samples of various types of the item you are looking at to your establishment to make it easier on you. This way you know exactly what you are getting.

After you have placed your order, it is good practice to make sure that what has been ordered has an open place on the shelves waiting for it when it arrives. A good thing to do is to label all of your shelves so others will know where things should be placed. Every product and item in your kitchen should have its own place for easy access and restock.

Now you are ready to receive the order. Whether you have been using the same vendor for a long time or not, it is always good practice to weigh, count, and open every box that comes through the back door if possible. Not every restaurant does this, so you need to warn your vendor that you will be doing this so they can schedule more time for your stop. The vendor will hand you an invoice for the following: product ordered, quantity at which it was ordered, and for what price it was ordered. Check this against the order sheet. If the order sheet is done correctly, then any other manager or supervisor should be able to check in the product. When checking in the product, you need to be as discerning as you can. Again, check size, weight, portion, and open every case to ensure that no damage was done and that the product quality is up to par. In the food cost control cycle, receiving and storage are points at which your restaurant is exposed to waste, theft, and spoilage. A successful manager acknowledges that these activities constitute a vital part of control. Properly trained employees must know the receiving procedures and have the right equipment. An accurately balanced set of scales for weighing the products and a dial thermometer to determine whether the proper temperatures have been maintained in the transportation of frozen foods and perishables may also come in handy.

Recap: Receiving Procedures

Before signing for receipt of the products, inspect them to ensure the following:

1. The item received is in good condition.

2. Weight or count shown on the invoice corresponds to both what was ordered and what was delivered. For example, a spec on a salmon may be 6 oz. If you accept salmon that exceeds the weight specs, you will have a higher food cost per order of salmon.

3. The quality of the products matches the specifications for that product. Careful inspection is geared more toward good business practice on the part of management than the integrity of the supplier. Mistakes can be made either by suppliers or by employees. Careful checking can eliminate or correct these mistakes.

4. If any items appear defective or substandard, return them and make the price changes on the invoice in the presence of the delivery personnel and have them sign against the returned items on the invoice.

5. Once you have conducted a satisfactory checking of the delivery, the invoice is signed and put in an assigned safe place for logging purposes.

6. The delivery is stored in the proper place immediately.

Quality of product, unfortunately, is something that many restaurants fail to sufficiently address when it comes through their back door. Remember, if you are receiving your orders early enough, then the vendor has time to take back anything you find unacceptable and return with replacement product the same day. If you do find something wrong with your order, whether you return it or not, it is always a good idea to call your representative and let them know of your disappointment. In some cases that is all it takes, and from there on out, your orders will be correct. In other cases, the rep may issue you a credit, even if you did use the product. This way they can keep your business and keep you happy.

Recap: Purchase of Product

A. Determine the quantity needed by utilizing proper order sheets—set accurate pars for ordering and prep to avoid under- or overstocking.

B. Place orders with those suppliers who offer the best quality at the lowest price.

C. Choose your vendors by:

1. The quality of the vendor's product—Study the variety of products available carefully to determine which one of them provides the best quality and yield for the money. It may take time to learn which supplier yields the best results, but it is time well spent in the long run.

2. Purveyor's price—Although as buyers we are often aware of the importance of considering the price of the products we buy, we sometimes fail to put price into proper perspective with other factors. Consequently, we sometimes put *too* much emphasis on buying the cheapest product and, as a result, actually end up paying more in terms of cost per portion (due to yield) and preparation time. In your market area, for example, there may be two or three suppliers of leaf lettuce, two of them consistently offering a case at a lower price than the third, but careful yield-testing of the lettuce may indicate that the company with the higher price really was offering the best buy (bigger heads with less waste and thus a more usable product for the total cost).

3. Vendor's service—The vendor who gives good service:

a. Delivers when your restaurant needs a shipment and is ready for it.

b. Keeps prices in line with the market and strives to maintain high standards of quality and service.

c. Acts as source of information about new products and other important developments in the market. The method for buying most food products is by competitive bidding. Get a list from each supplier of the major items and then award the day's (periods) purchases according to the lowest *net cost per order*. If you use this method correctly and consistently, especially on foods whose prices fluctuate over short periods of time (e.g., seafood, some produce) you will work toward an ideal food cost.

Now, that your product is in the restaurant, it needs to be put away in the proper place, at the proper temperatures, and adhering to all Health Department regulations.

Once the product starts to be pulled from the shelves, you need to try to monitor its every move. The importance of watching over your employees while they are prepping, storing, cooking, and serving can make or break your food cost.

A few chapters back, we briefly discussed pricing out recipes and plate cost. Now let us take a look at this in greater depth. Say you budget your food cost at a 30.5% (as shown in 2.1). Not all restaurants will budget their food cost at the same percentage. In fact, 30.5% is high. Most restaurants average 28% to 30%. If you have an Italian, Mexican, Pizza, or fast-food concept, you could set your food cost in the low twenties. Of course, there are exceptions to this rule. If you have a concept that is an upscale restaurant, perhaps selling some higher-ticket items (like some seafood or steak), then you would need to set your food cost a little higher.

Food Cost (in relation to a menu item) is generated from the amount of money spent on a particular product or recipe to create a menu item. This is then taken against the amount of money the item is being sold for on the menu, to end up with a percentage that equals cents to the dollar. Say I want to have salmon on the menu. I will top it off with a white wine cream sauce and pour sautéed garlic, mushrooms, and baby shrimp over my sauce. I will serve it with a vegetable medley and rice pilaf. If I put this description on my menu, I must put a price along with it. How can I figure out what my cost should be? This process of fixing prices to menu items or specials should not be a guessing game. You should never hear a chef say, "Let's sell the special today at $16.95—no, wait, $12.95. Well what do you think?" All items should be priced out. On your menu, or even with your specials, you may find you have some menu items that are way above your budgeted food cost, some that are well below, and some that hit it right on. Your first reaction may be to cut back on some portions to lower the cost or maybe just delete the higher-cost (products that costs you a lot of money compared to the price you sell them for) items from the menu. Do not do this. The higher-cost menu items, most of the time, will be offset by your lower-cost menu items. Your higher-cost items, like seafood, steak, game, or any other hard-to-get item may be the thing that are separating you from the other restaurants. As long as you have higher-, medium-, and lower-end items, you will be able to please a wider variety of clientele. The relation between higher-cost items and lower-cost items stems from food cost. Let me give you an example of what a higher-cost item is. Say you have just the salmon on the menu by itself that costs you $2.43 and sells for $11.95. In the same turn, say you have some cheesecake on the menu that costs the restaurant $1.25 a slice and sells for $4.95. Normally, you would automatically think the salmon would be a higher-cost item because it costs more to get it in the restaurant. However, the cheesecake is actually the higher-cost item, because it makes less of a profit. Remember, the cost of an item is in relation to food cost.

5.2 Higher-cost Items

$2.43 (cost for salmon)	$1.25 (cost for cheesecake)
÷ $11.95 (menu price)	÷ $4.95 (menu price)
20% (food cost)	25% (food cost)

The customer will only pay so much for a certain item. Any restaurant should make the guest feel they are getting their money's worth. Not many people want to pay more than $11.95 for a plain salmon or $4.95 for a slice of cheesecake. This means that you are stuck in this price range for the item. In 5.2, you see that higher cost is directly related to the restaurant's food cost. To the customer, in 5.2, the salmon is the higher-cost item because it costs them more. For the restaurant, the cheesecake is the higher-cost item because it cost $0.25 on the dollar to sell the cheesecake and only $0.20 on the dollar to sell the salmon.

If you have items on your menu that are 16% to 20% and 26% to 34% in food cost, you are creating a balance to your menu. This balance should have you hit your budgeted food cost around 28% to 30%. The only thing that will determine your overall balance is the product mix (P-mix) report. This name varies from concept to concept. Some call it the *menu item count*. P-mix *is the total amounts of each menu item or drink sold for a particular period of time.* The P-mix can help you in many different ways. This report can help you decide if you want to keep a certain menu item, find out whether you have waste or theft, and find out why your food cost may be too high or too low. By looking at the P-mix report for the month, you can see how much of an item has been sold. If you have a menu item that only sold once or twice the whole month, you may want to change the item. You can also compare the inventory of how many pieces of salmon you bought against how many were sold to find out whether there is a discrepancy. If there is, you need to then check into the possibility of waste (items that go bad and need to be thrown away) or theft. For these reasons, your food cost could be going up. Looking at this report can also show you, in some cases if you are selling a lot more higher-dollar items, whether this could be the reason your food cost is up.

One other thing that this report can do for you is to help you set par levels. If the report says you are only selling ten turkeys a week, then there is no reason for you to keep buying a case of twenty a week and having ten of them go to waste.

Getting back to salmon and how you are going to price it, unfortunately, there is no short way of creating a menu cost. You must take the menu item and dissect every part. First, the salmon…

5.3 Costing Out the Salmon

$48.50 (one 10-lb. side of salmon)
÷   10 (the number of pounds of salmon)
   $4.85   4.85 (what each pound cost)
                        ÷   2 (16 oz. in a pound, and I want half)
                        $2.43 (cost for 8-oz. portion)

In 5.3 you can see I have found out the cost per salmon that will be served on the menu. I bought the salmon in a 10-pound portion and decided I wanted to serve an 8-ounce portion on my menu. I must find out the cost per pound first, and then I can find out the cost of each 8-ounce portion. If I were to serve a 10-ounce portion, I would need to find out what each ounce costs and then multiply by 10.

5.4 Costing Out 10-Ounce Portion of Salmon

$4.85 (what each pound cost me)
÷   16 (16 oz. in every pound)
   .30   .30 (cost per ounce)
                     ×   10 (10-oz. portion)
                     $3.00 (cost for 10-oz. portion)

5.5 Cost for 4 Ounces of White Wine Cream Sauce

White Wine Cream Sauce   **Yields 1 Quart**

Item	Unit Size	Unit Cost	Recipe Portion	Recipe Cost
Heavy Cream	1 qt.	1.09	1 qt.	1.09
Milk	1 gal.	2.29	2 cups	0.29
White Wine	1 5-gal. Box	18.95	1/2 cup	0.12
Butter	1 lb.	0.99	1/2 lb	0.5
Garlic	1 qt.	1.14	2 tbs.	0.02
Flour	1 lb.	0.89	2 tbs.	0.05
Onion	1 gal.	1.89	1 cup	0.12
Shrimp Base	1 lb.	9.29	1 tsp	0.23
White Pepper	1 lb.	4.26	1 tsp	0.11
Oregano	1 lb.	4.89	1 tsp	0.12
Basil	1 lb.	4.68	1 tsp	0.12

Total Cost to Make the Sauce: 2.77
Cost for 4 oz. of Sauce: 0.35

In 5.5 I have taken the sauce that will go on the fish, broken down the recipe, and found that one recipe costs $2.77. I then took the yield of 1 quart and divided by how many half-cups (4 oz.) are in a quart (8). I then took the total cost to make the sauce and divided by 8 to come up with the cost for 4 ounces of sauce ($0.35). In order to break down recipes, it is always good to have the latest cost for the unit size from your vendor, the recipe unit measure, and a portion chart that will show you the breakdown of certain measurements. (If you use Red Books for your manager notebook, you may find a chart inside.) Take your recipe and chart it out similar to the one in 5.5. *Unit Size* pertains to the size of the product when it came in from the vendor to you. This could equal a case, gallon, weight, quart, sack, or a variety of other ways you may get the product from your vendor. *Unit Cost* pertains to the amount of money you paid for the Unit Size. In 5.5, a gallon of milk costs $2.29. *Recipe Portion* refers to the amount of the Unit Size of a particular product we will be putting in our recipe. Out of the gallon of milk, only two cups will be used. *Recipe Cost* is found by taking how many times your Recipe Portion will go into your Unit Size. Then take the Unit Cost and divide it by the number you got. For milk I take the one gallon of milk and divide by how many times 2 cups go into a gallon. It will go into a gallon 8 times (a gallon has 16 cups, and therefore 2 cups goes into it 8 times). We then take the Unit Cost of $2.29 and divide it by 8 to end up with our Recipe Cost of $0.29.

$2.29 (cost for a gallon of milk)

÷   8 (number of times 2 cups go into a gallon)

.29 (cost, in milk, for this recipe)

Once you have reached a recipe cost for everything in the recipe, you then add the recipe cost column together and put your total at the bottom, as seen in 5.5. Now that you have your cost for how much a full recipe yields, you must then break this down to the portion size you will be using for the menu item. On the salmon, I want to put 4 ounces of sauce. We then need to take the yield of 1 quart and find out how many times 4 ounces will go into it. There are 32 ounces in a quart (or 4 cups). There are 8 ounces in a cup. This is the same procedure that we just went over with the Recipe Cost. After dividing 4 into 32 and then dividing $2.77 (cost of total recipe) by 8, I then end up with the menu cost portion for the sauce of $0.35.

These are the procedures and steps you should take for the vegetable medley, rice pilaf, and toppings. Once you have all of the costs, you will then need to add them all together. Remember, I am doing all of these steps to find out the price to put on one menu item.

5.6 Food Cost for the Salmon Menu Item

8 oz. Salmon	$2.43
4 oz. Wine Sauce	$0.35
3 oz. Topping	
(Garlic, Mushrooms, Baby Shrimp)	$0.85
4 oz. Rice Pilaf	$0.45
4 oz. Vegetable Medley	$0.35
Total amount it will cost us to make this menu it	$4.43
If we want our plate cost to be a 28% food cost, we will then take 4.43 and divide it by 28% to get:	**$15.82**

**Note: This is the amount we should charge
on the menu for this particular item.**

In 5.6, I have shown you how to get your menu cost for a particular item. If you want the guest to pay less money for this item, then you would simply up your food-cost percentage.

$4.43 (the amount it cost to make this item)

÷   0.30 (30% food cost to hit)

$14.77 (the amount the guest should pay on the menu)

Now that I have cost-out a recipe, it is easy to see why it is so important for your employees to follow them. A few chapters back I discussed the importance of knowing each position, how it feels to be that particular employee who has to peel shrimp for many hours, and how they can become easily distracted, tired, or bored. With the employees who are making the recipes, it is the same thing. They, too, get bored doing the same recipes over and over. Some feel they know the recipe so well, because they have done it so many times that they do not need the recipe book or cards in front of them. I suggest you make sure they are always looking at the recipe, even if they have done it thousands of times. If you feel you can trust them, that is fine, too, but you should quiz them every so often. I think you will be amazed at the results.

It is also important to make sure the employee is using the proper measuring tools. I have seen over and over where the employee will guess what equals a cup, or how much 11.5 pounds is. A common problem in kitchens is a lack of tools. The employee tries to get through the work given to them in the amount of time given to them, but has to stop and wait for someone else to get through using the tool they need or has to spend time looking for the tool. This can be very frustrating, especially for the more fragile recipes where timing is everything. As a manager, you are responsible for ensuring that there are tools to use and a place to put them. Storing your tools can be challenging when you do not know who used them last and when you have many of them. Just like the food that comes through the back door or the plates that go up on the line, you need to have a home for your tools, a place where they go after being cleaned so that anyone can find and use them at any time.

Food cost can be the most challenging category under cost of sales. There are so many factors that need to be considered when producing a good food cost. In addition, even if you do hit your budgeted food cost, it does not necessarily mean you have produced the best cost possible. Remember, your budget is just a target percentage to hit. One way to see your food cost results is to constantly analyze your food by doing inventories.

Profitability is determined by how well you control your food cost. Food cost is the single most significant cost in a restaurant. In addition to the direct cost of purchased food items, there are associated costs including handling, storage, and labor. It is understood that a manager's ultimate personal success and that of a restaurant may be determined by how effectively you control your food cost.

Food cost is generally computed as a total dollar cost and stated as a percentage of food sales.

Food cost for any weekly or monthly period can be determined by inserting the appropriate information into the following equation.

Beginning Inventory + Your Purchases – Ending Inventory = Food Cost

Beginning Inventory = *for one accounting period is the ending inventory for the one preceding it.*

Purchases = *the dollar amount of total items purchased for the period.*

Ending Inventory = *the physical count of the food items on hand multiplied by the cost of each item.*

The food cost percentage involves stating the food cost as a percentage of food sales, which equals cents on the dollar. To do this, you simply take your food cost and divide it by your food sales. The food cost percentage is then used both as a budgeting tool and as a measure of performance. A rise in food cost percentage indicates that there is a problem and action must be taken to determine exactly what product's usage is out of line. Generally, a significant variation in food cost results from purchasing the wrong product (wrong specification items), poor receiving procedures (not counting, weighing, or checking quality), poor storage (wrong temperature, poor sanitation), over-portioning, or theft.

Look at some ideas you need to think about when storing your goods. In the overall operation of a kitchen, storage forms an important link between receiving and final presentation. The quality of a storage system, therefore, directly affects the quality of the product you use in food preparation. It represents one aspect of an operation where, as a manager, you can exert effective control by eliminating shrinkage, spoilage, and theft to help keep food cost down.

Loss from shrinkage mainly occurs with meats and produce through exposure to the dry air in the refrigerators. To avoid this, ensure that food items are covered or wrapped tightly while in storage. More importantly, keep the quantity of stored items at a minimum to facilitate timely usage.

Spoilage is largely the result of the growth of microorganisms in unprocessed foods. Proper temperature controls in storage areas and good sanitation help slow down the growth of microorganisms and consequently prevent spoilage. Perishable items should be stored immediately after delivery.

For normal refrigerator temperature, you should maintain between 35°F and 40°F. Produce, meat, and seafood should be slightly lower, at 32°F to 35°F, to help prolong their quality and appearance. Frozen food (e.g., shrimp, wings, ice cream, fries, etc.) should be stored in its original carton, immediately after delivery, and at 0°F. For nonrefrigerated items, you can store products at a relative humidity of 50% to 60% and no more. When you arrange your storage room, a good rule of thumb is to store frequently used items where they can be reached easily and stock foods of the same kind together.

Use the first-in, first-out method (FIFO). Always move the older stock to the front of the shelves and put the new stock in the back. A trick I have used in the past is to cross-stack such items as potatoes and flour in alternating patterns on skids or racks. Store food away from the walls and off the floor at least six inches (the Health Department requires this). Do not get too tight in your coolers. You should always allow air circulation around products. To make it more efficient, you should store heavier items close to the floor. Do not store food in the same area as your chemicals. Provide separate storage for nonfood items that give off fumes, such as cleaning agents and paint.

Ways to Extend Shelf Life with Good Sanitation Practices

The cleaning of storerooms and refrigerators represents one aspect of a program to extend the shelf life of food. Bacteria cling to particles of food and multiply on shelving, from which they can be transferred to foods. Therefore, sanitation in the storage areas should be specified and scheduled. The following rules will help you devise an adequate cleaning schedule:

- Wash walk-in coolers and refrigerators daily.
- Place thawing meats on racks above pans.
- Remove spoiled food immediately.

- Sweep storeroom floors daily. Mop the floors with disinfectant. Wash walls, storage shelves, and storeroom equipment on a regular basis.
- Use ice bags to keep thawed out and prepped seafood within safe temperature ranges.
- Use professional services for pest control.
- Schedule freezer defrosting when the quantity of food is at its lowest level.
- Periodically call in a competent refrigeration mechanic or set up a monthly HVAC contract to check the compressors, condensers, and motors on all your reach-in refrigerators, walk-in refrigerators, and freezers.
- Inspect storeroom areas regularly.

Some Ways to Use Security and Food Storage

- Large losses of food through pilferage (theft) can be reflected in an increase in food cost or an unusual variance in inventory. However, petty pilferage—the kind employees do not consider as such—may be difficult to detect, and storage and storeroom controls must be used to keep it to a minimum.
- The physical arrangement and the management of storage areas can reduce pilferage greatly. In most cases, maximum-security storage areas, especially for expensive items like lobster and shrimp, should be identified as such and be equipped with special locks that limit access to a few people. Remember how we talked about locking up your linen? Well, this is the same thing. Most restaurants will now have meat cages. This is a good method of control and helps maintain food cost.
- The back door should be locked at all times and no food should be allowed to go out the back door.

- Use daily meat and seafood inventory sheets to inventory and keep track of the variance in usage of these expensive items and facilitate speed in detecting pilferage.

- Have a strict policy of promptly dealing with anyone who you catch stealing from you. In most cases, if you are with a big company and had caught someone stealing from you, you must call the corporate office for guidance.

Some Good Ways to Control Food Cost through Tight Controls and Planning

In food service, there are certain variables that may affect the operation of a kitchen. If a manager fails to identify, study, and predict these variables, he or she may be faced with drastic changes in food sales that may send food cost sky high. An easy way to summarize these variables is to look at time, weather, and special conditions.

- **Time:** Sales volume varies with time

Know the busiest and slowest hours of the day, days of the week, and seasons of the year and adjust your ordering and prepping accordingly. Predictions or peak volume time periods, whether in terms of months or of ten-minute segments, generally are made on the basis of historical records. Daily reports will provide data that can be summarized for each day of the week. Monthly sales can be compiled from daily reports.

- **Weather:**

The effect of weather on sales depends on where the restaurant is, who its customers are, and how the customers' preferences are affected by weather. By gathering information, you can study business trends as they vary with the weather and then *avoid* unnecessary overpreparation of food. An example of this would be if you owned a restaurant in a ballpark. You should assume you would be much busier during baseball season and order more than when baseball is out of season.

- **Special Conditions:**

Be aware of scheduled local events like parades and conventions. If you do have events in your local area it is good practice to call the surrounding hotels and find out how full they will be. Obtain a guaranteed number of guests in banquets. Anticipate the possibility of overattendance and always confirm the dates and times of banquets with the organizers at least three days before the event. It is always a good idea to plan ahead for holidays like Thanksgiving and Mother's Day or any other holiday that may be celebrated in your area.

- **Portion Control:**

All the care taken in planning and production of food can be defeated if food is prepped and served without controls. If your kitchen over-portions 10 ounces of crabmeat by only 1/2 ounce, 5% of the product is wasted. Remember I said that an average restaurant will only make four cents on the dollar, or 4%. Therefore, since 4% commonly represents the profit margin of a successful restaurant, the significance of portion control should be obvious. Portion control is also important in maintaining customer goodwill. If you overportion one time to a guest, and the next time you underportion, you will turn off the guest and they may not return. In most chain restaurants, the portion sizes for food have been specified in a plate presentation manual, based on food cost and guest satisfaction. Always use the manual if you work for a corporate restaurant and ensure that your employees understand the importance of serving the correct portions on plates.

Some Ways to Ensure the Use of Tools for Portion Control

A key to successful portion control is the correct and consistent use of standardized recipes. Variations in recipes could reduce or increase amount of ingredients. Involvement of all managers in support of strict portion-control procedures will accomplish much in controlling food cost. The managers' random weighing of lettuce bags, portioning of chicken, counting of shrimp portions, et cetera will demonstrate the seriousness of the issue to employees. Management's approach should be to insist upon the specified portion size for every thing.

Some Things Your Kitchen Should Never Be Without:

- Balanced ounce and pound scales
- Specified-size ladles, scoops, spatulas, and other utensils
- Some method of dating your product
- Portion bags and containers with lids
- Linens (e.g., towels and aprons)

You should not only ensure adequate availability of such tools, but also ensure that they are used consistently. Although experienced cooks can follow directions, they may not in fact do so. Even experienced cooks need supervision to ensure that care is taken.

Some Ways to Control Waste

- Attain maximum yield of products during preparation.
- Discourage overpeeling or overtrimming of items such as onions and lettuce.
- Ensure that only minimal waste is discarded when cutting off roots from celery and green onion.
- Inspect all items thrown into food-waste containers. Look for items that could have been used but were not (the last few strawberries in a pint, the leftover half tomato, the extra leaf of lettuce, etc.). I have gone as far as having my cooks throw all their waste into their own clear Cambro container so I can see who is throwing away what.
- Ensure that sauce and dressing containers are scraped with rubber spatulas.
- Ensure accurate par levels and prep lists to eliminate overprepping of food items.
- All items should be prepared fresh daily so that the shelf life of the product is not exceeded.
- Use waste sheets to record uncooked products or items wasted through mistakes or miscommunication.

- Emphasize good storage and rotation procedures by consistent use-of-day dots (or any dating method) and labeling.

- Train your employees to use ice baths to quickly cool down soups and sauces.

- Study your "voids" and "comps" every day to see if there is a pattern of mistakes by the kitchen or service personnel, and discuss such mistakes with your employees on a ongoing basis with the purpose of eliminating as many mistakes as possible.

- Ensure the accuracy of your inventory by assigning two managers to do the counting and recording of products on hand.

- Ensure that your employees have good cooking and food-handling habits, and that their hair is well groomed and covered.

- Carefully plan your daily specials and cost them out to enhance overall food cost.

- Maintain a current price list of all food items you buy, especially seafood, dairy, and produce, and ensure that the correct prices are used when costing specials and extending inventory for cost of sales.

- Monitor and control the preparation of salads to discourage overprepping. Prepped salad mix must be kept dry and refrigerated to avoid spoilage.

- Plan workable methods of controlling preparation of precooked items like bread, baked potatoes, vegetables, rice, beans, and sauces. Such items should be held on the line at the minimum needed at a time. Replenish as you go.

- Insist on control over manager and employee meals. If you are giving free or discounted food to your managers and staff, make sure they are not eating your higher cost items. Also do not let them eat a lot in one sitting. I have seen and used a smaller menu comprised of menu items that are not high in cost or hard to prep.

- Food items that are handled by service personnel should be monitored closely. Discourage unnecessary preparation of too much coffee or tea during slow periods. Turn off some of the coffee and tea machines.

- If your servers make their own salads rather than getting them from the kitchen, train the servers to properly portion dressings, croutons, and cheese. Servers should not combine salads to make them larger. I have witnessed some servers using twice the correct portion size to make salad for customers who request a larger salad.

- Portioning of fries at the fry station should be taken as seriously as portioning of any other food items. Fries are among the most heavily used items in most kitchens. Fry cooks must be trained to drop only as many fries as needed to cover existing orders and no more.

- Train your fry cooks to sift and reuse seasoned flour through the day.

- Train your cooks to obtain as much usable product as they can when cutting and cleaning produce such as onions, tomatoes, cucumbers, bell peppers, celery, green onions, and lettuce. Check garbage cans periodically to ensure this.

- Check the line regularly to make sure that cold, perishable items are held at appropriate temperature and that they are sanitary and not waterlogged.

- Pay specific attention to seafood and other frozen products that are commonly thawed out in sinks under running water. Ensure that such products are not left forgotten in the sinks all day. Delicate items such as shrimp and fish will quickly go bad if left at room temperature or under water for an extended amount of time. Implement a workable pull thaw system to avoid such occurrences.

- Filter fryer oil at the end of every shift

- Shake excess water off items before dropping in a fryer to extend the life of your frying oil.

Some Ways to Find Out Why Your Cost Is Rising

- If your cost of sales indicates a rise in food cost, the rise clearly signals a problem. Necessary steps must be taken to trace the problem.

- Remember the equation for computing food cost?

  Beginning Inventory + Purchases – Ending Inventory = Cost of Sale

1. There may be a mistake in the beginning inventory figure used to compute the current food cost.

2. Compare your current beginning inventory with the ending inventory of the previous accounting period. They should be the same.

3. There may be a mistake in the total amount of current invoices or purchases.

4. Total up the amounts on current invoices to determine purchases. Did you miss an invoice?

5. There may be a mistake in ending inventory.

6. Confirm the accuracy of your most recent inventory and check the validity of the prices used to extend the inventory to a dollar amount.

7. If you are using a computer program to produce your cost of sales, check the formulas in the program for accuracy.

If these steps do not expose the problem, then the discrepancy is likely to have arisen from waste of an expensive and heavily used product or a combination of products. Products such as shrimp, meat, and other heavily used items may cause great damage to your food cost if not closely controlled.

- Use your product mix to find out the use of high-volume, high-cost menu items.

- Once you locate the problem product, take quick and immediate action to remedy the situation as outlined above.

*If you are experiencing a food-cost problem for which you do not have a solution, *never* manipulate the figures to make it look better.

Epilogue

$$$

Time to Crunch Some Numbers

Knowing how to control your restaurant dollars is not only smart; it makes you more money. Why would you not want to know how to make your restaurant and yourself more profitable? Even if you are an entry-level manager, it is important that you understand the value of every dollar that is made at the restaurant.

I once was told by a CEO of a major company that he felt this book was good but that it was basic and did not really teach him anything he did not already know. After I stopped laughing to myself, I told him as politely as I could that, if he learned anything from this book, I would have to question his position as a CEO for a major restaurant chain. He finally understood the importance of a book like this when one of his restaurants ran short on management and the company had to promote two bartenders at the restaurant. Neither of the bartenders had been in management before but understood how to treat guests and train employees. This company was about to have two green managers and one seasoned manager run a startup concept in an 8,400-square foot restaurant. More than half the management team did not even understand what the CEO was saying when he mentioned that he wanted to increase the "top line" and that eventually they would have to get tighter on the "bottom line."

This is where I stepped in to help out. First, I made sure the two managers knew the importance of taking care of the employees. Without employees, we would not be able to operate. Second, we trained them on taking care of the guests. Without the guests, we would not need to be here. These first two steps were pretty easy with all the available literature there is today to teach any seasoned or entry-level manager on how to think, feel, act, react, respond, ignore, and handle any and all guests, employees, and situations that should arise on a given shift. The third and last thing I taught the managers was the importance of number crunching. Without being profitable, we would eventually end up closing our doors and not need to worry about taking care of our employees or our guest. The only way to become profitable is to understand how to crunch numbers. This is where I set up one day each week to meet and go over each chapter of this book. After we learned a new subject, I gave them homework that related to the restaurant they were running at that time. Like I said before, not all schedules, P&Ls, and so forth look the same, and the one at their restaurant looked completely different from the one in this book. On the days we met we read the materials, I would show them how to work out some of the problems on an ongoing work tablet we had, then we reviewed the information and did situational examples. Does this method sound familiar?

Tell, show, do, review is the best way to teach anything. When one is training someone they should always use the tell, show, do, review method to help the person learning really comprehend what it is they are learning about. First you must tell them what you want them to learn and explain (or in our case we read the chapter) what the results or outcome will be. Next you show them how to do the task. Then you have them do the exact thing you just taught them to make sure they actually understand what they just learned. The final thing is to review and talk again about each step to drill it in a little more. It amazes me how well this method works if used correctly. When I teach employees to become trainers, I use this method in our classes and then have the employees come up with something they are going to teach the class. It is a great lesson. When we teach someone else, we may leave out some of the details because we take for granted our knowledge about the subject and assume how much the other person already knows. I remember a time when I managed a restaurant in Memphis with four other managers and made such an assumption. I gave a task to one of my managers to sand down a piano and refinish it. I assigned the task and did nothing more. I assumed the manager did not need me to tell, show, do, and review with him. Surely, he had sanded and stained wood before. A week had gone by and the task was not complete. When I approached the manager about it, he just said he did not have time and that he would get it done within the next week. Another week went by and the piano was still not touched. I was getting impatient and disappointed. I sat the manager down and asked him what was going on. He confessed he was embarrassed to tell me he did not know how to sand a piano, much less stain it. He said he went to the store to buy sandpaper and there were so many various grades and sizes, not to mention the different kinds of stains. It really taught me a lesson I will never forget. When people do not understand how to do things that other people assume they should know how to do, they may pretend to know. This is the case with plenty of managers.

In the case of the entry-level managers I was teaching number-crunching with, I found that tell, show, do, review worked great. In fact, the restaurant had been open for three-and-a-half years and never turned a profit, but after just six-and-a-half months of being managers and knowing how to crunch numbers, the restaurant was up 7% in comp store sales and had had its first period ever to show a profit. I believe the concept and the new managers have a bright future and long road of success ahead.

I know not everyone likes to crunch numbers. Unfortunately, you need to be able to do it in this career and to be successful. As I said before, numbers do not create themselves; we create the numbers through everything we do on a daily basis. Crunching numbers in a restaurant is the difference between unsuccessful and successful managers and general managers.